Transforming
the Culture
of
School
Leadership

Some people come into our lives and quietly go; others stay for a while and leave footprints on our heart; and we are never the same.

—Anonymous

We dedicate this book to all educators whose compassion guides their journey . . . and to Leslie.

—J. G. & J. H.

Transforming *the* Culture *of* School Leadership

Humanizing Our Practice

JOSEPH M. GIANCOLA
JANICE K. HUTCHISON
Foreword by
Richard Hawthorne

CORWIN PRESS
A SAGE Publications Company
Thousand Oaks, California

Illustrations by Wendy Coy.

For information:

Corwin Press
A Sage Publications Company
2455 Teller Road
Thousand Oaks, California 91320
www.corwinpress.com

Sage Publications Ltd.
1 Oliver's Yard
55 City Road
London EC1Y 1SP
United Kingdom

Sage Publications India Pvt. Ltd.
B-42, Panchsheel Enclave
Post Box 4109
New Delhi 110 017 India

Printed in the United States of America

Library of Congress Cataloging-in-Publication Data

Giancola, Joseph M.
Transforming the culture of school leadership: Humanizing our practice / Joseph M. Giancola and Janice K. Hutchison.
    p. cm.
Includes bibliographical references and index.
ISBN 1-4129-1609-7 (cloth) — ISBN 1-4129-1610-0 (pbk.)
   1. Educational leadership—Philosophy. 2. School management and organization—Philosophy. I. Hutchison, Janice K. II. Title.
LB2805.G427 2005
371.2—dc22

                                                    2004028781

This book is printed on acid-free paper.

05   06   07   08   09   10   9   8   7   6   5   4   3   2   1

Acquisitions Editor:	Elizabeth Brenkus
Editorial Assistant:	Candice L. Ling
Production Editor:	Melanie Birdsall
Copy Editor:	Terese Platten, Freelance Editorial Services
Typesetter:	C&M Digitals (P) Ltd.
Proofreader:	Cheryl Rivard
Indexer:	Sheila Bodell
Cover Designer:	Rose Storey
Graphic Designer:	Lisa Miller

Contents

Foreword

What a joy to read a book about education leadership that brings research, theory, and a spiritual perspective to bear on the realities of school life. In this very valuable piece of work, Joseph M. Giancola and Janice K. Hutchison have set out a straightforward challenge: How might we interrupt the *power over* untrusting, self-protecting, and other inhibiting features so evident in the lives of professionals in far too many of our schools? The concern about such features is that the ways teachers and principals frame, deliberate over, make decisions about, and act on the problematics of teaching and learning directly affect the quality of life and learning for students. For this reason, they offer a compelling alternative way to think about and enact professional leadership in schools.

They set out in clear terms an image of schools (and districts) centered by a humane approach to the work at hand. They do so by integrating research, both their own and from the body of inquiry about organizational life with theories about adult learning, power allocations, trusting relationships, and an ethic of caring and principles of a strong democracy. Through this vantage point, they invite the reader to consider bringing a Humane Dimension to school leadership as they create and sustain a transformative school culture.

If you have had the opportunity to visit a number of schools during the instructional day, you remember some because you saw principals and teachers talking about curriculum and teaching or about some accomplishment a student or group experienced, or about an issue facing them. They listened to each other, sought out each other's views, and respected and trusted one another even when they disagreed. The focus was student well-being and learning. These are but a few of the markers of a school in which the professional life is transformational in character.

By *transformational* is meant the ongoing growth of individuals and organizations through the continuous examination of our beliefs and the behaviors we exhibit in our workplaces and with each other. This is not a pathological exercise directed toward finding out what is wrong and fixing it; rather, it is a process of learning and problem solving with each other to enrich the quality of life and learning in the school. It is transformational because the professionals are in the continuous process of reframing the problems and issues that define each school day. They do not assume that there is but one way or one authority who has the answers. It is transformational because these efforts at constructing meaningful educational programs and practices are grounded in principles of pedagogy, democracy, and caring. The Humane Dimension of transformative schools is that set of principles and behaviors that form the passion we invoke as we work together in this important effort called education.

I, as have many readers, have worked in organizations that lacked sufficient humaneness or transformational qualities, and I have worked in some that gave meaning to those same qualities. Indeed, I probably have contributed to both the lack and hopefully the presence of these growth-fostering conditions. It is far more meaningful and productive to work in the transformative setting where colleagues prize the insights and perspectives of each other and care enough to deliberate with honesty and passion over matters of consequence.

To be transformational and enact an ethic of caring does not mean all is quiet and peaceful. Indeed, there is wonderful growth involved when we bring the best of our diverse minds to the examination of what happens in classrooms, in curriculum design and development deliberations, and in rethinking our assumptions about students and how they learn. To honestly engage the issues and problems necessarily means that differences of belief and reasoning will emerge. The challenge in a professional culture is to engage the issues and problems openly and fully while also caring about others and demonstrating democratic principles in action (i.e., full regard for diversity, for deep deliberation, and for consensus building—the win/win perspective described in Chapter 6 of this book).

Building trusting relationships is very hard to do in a place controlled by top-down expectations, by undermining and self-serving conduct, and by a lack of celebration of successes. But it is doable. Indeed, this book is filled with ways to initiate collaborative problem solving, joint planning of curriculum and professional development, and consensus building. I am particularly pleased with the curriculum-centered professional development section in Chapter 7. Indeed, one could argue that the entire work is curriculum centered.

Another valuable aspect of this work is the array of rich resources the authors have brought to bear as they set out their perspective and illustrate what the emerging practices can be.

Finally, although they illustrate the principles and constructs of their perspective on leadership, the authors do not prescribe simplistic rules or practices. Indeed, they close several chapters with questions designed to invite the reader to imagine how humane leadership and transformative cultures might play out in their own school contexts. How appropriate to use questions rather than rules of conduct.

Joe and Janice bring extensive experience and thoughtfulness to this work. They are not pie-in-the-sky people who think that if we are just nice to each other, everything will be fine. They are tough-minded, thoroughly grounded in theory, research, and practice, and street-smart about the ideas they ask us to consider. What is so refreshing is that they center their effort on the Humane Dimension. They ask us to be mature professionals and care about each other as we wrestle with the problematics of school life and educational activity. This is why this book is so valuable to all of us.

—*Richard Hawthorne*

Preface

As teachers in public schools, each of us has been educating our students for more than 25 years. Much of this time has been spent in the Kent City School District in Kent, Ohio. Between the two of us, we have more than 50 years of classroom and school experience.

As practitioners and observers of changes in public schools, we have been researching and writing about our observations and findings for only the past 16 years. While completing our doctoral studies and teaching in the evenings at Kent State University, we have concluded that there is a dimension of teaching, learning, and leading that should be described in writing. Numerous observations made and relationships formed in several school districts convinced us that this dimension deserved credence. We were compelled to write this book to give this dimension a name, a description, and a place in our peers' work toward meaningful school change; by doing so, we have defined a destination toward which we all should move to transform school culture. We call this dimension the *Humane Dimension—a place in an organization where personal transformation is allowed to occur in a culture of compassion, trust, empowering relationships, and common purposes.*

Our studies began in 1988, when we explored the perceptions of stake-holders who were involved in their school's budgeting and decision-making processes. Decisions about a range of topics (e.g., curricular programs, personnel, and budgeting of resources) were explored in an attempt to understand how stakeholders' involvement could improve final decisions and outcomes of the educational process. At the same time, Theodore Roosevelt High School in Kent, Ohio, was thriving as an exemplar of school reform that had not yet been noted as such in the literature by any other researchers. It was during the 1984–1985 school year that Roosevelt High School was recognized by the U.S. Department of Education with the prestigious Excellence in Education award, then under the leadership of Principal Marty Kane.

After our first major study, we decided to focus our efforts on the staff, students, and parents of Theodore Roosevelt High School in 1993. We wanted to develop local knowledge (Cochran-Smith, 1993) about the effectiveness of its programs. We began a series of action research projects to describe, document, and assess the school reform efforts of Roosevelt's teachers and administrators. In 1997, we investigated the perceptions of five classroom teachers who were engaged in reform activities at Theodore Roosevelt High School. These five teacher reformers were facilitating four major reform projects in their school. Our study's research question focused on how power relations in the school affected their reform activities. A critical recommendation that resulted from this study is that power in schools must be reconceptualized as a relational concept characterized by parity and reciprocity.

After 1997, action research projects continued, and Theodore Roosevelt High School's growth increasingly became our focus. As we note in Chapter 1, the precise, cyclical nature of the Humane Dimension had become clear to us because of the natural flow of events during such a time of change in Roosevelt's history. By 2002, we had completed the first draft of the present book. We proceeded to conduct focus groups with teachers and administrators on both the components of the Humane Dimension and the elements of the transformed leadership and teacher cultures that we observed and later reported in our work. Excerpts from the focus group notes are featured throughout the book in sidebars called "Focus Group Response." During the 2003–2004 school year, the process of appreciative inquiry (Cooperrider & Whitney, 1999) was used to evaluate Roosevelt's past and to decide its future direction. At the time of this writing, enormous amounts of data that corroborate the cyclical nature of the Humane Dimension's four components have been collected at Roosevelt. Many of our subjects' comments contained in this book have been included.

We hope that this book will answer several important questions. The following list is not exhaustive but is a good beginning.

Q: How does the Humane Dimension relate to standards-based education?

A: The Humane Dimension describes a new context for educators to grow and to address the standards with renewed spirit.

Q: Is the Humane Dimension a theory?

A: No, it is a construct that we have developed. The four components (i.e., Communications Based on Trust, Empowering Relationships, Other-Centered Purpose, and Personal Transformation) are connected by a recursive cycle, which forms a foundation for organizational transformation.

Q: Is the Humane Dimension a cure for the many ills and challenges faced by educators?

A: No, it is one small piece of the complex puzzle of school reform. Many researchers clearly have made recommendations, which when used collectively, could underpin significant changes in public education.

School leaders—traditional administrators *and* teachers—will benefit from learning about the Humane Dimension and how to incorporate it into their practice. Educators and graduate students in areas of administration, curriculum, and instructional leadership may also find our humanistic approach a welcome addition to their courses.

Chapter 1, which defines the Humane Dimension, is followed by a chapter on each of its four components (i.e., Chapter 2, Communication Based on Trust; Chapter 3, Empowering Relationships; Chapter 4, Other-Centered Purpose; and Chapter 5, Personal and Organizational Transformation). Chapters 6 and 7 present the results of applying the Humane Dimension, namely, elements of transformed leadership and teacher cultures, respectively. Chapter 8, Handling Challenges and Pitfalls, advises readers on how to face their challenges or problems and deal with failure. Chapter 9, Evidence of the Humane Dimension in Schools, actually brings closure to the book and to the question of how to recognize the Humane Dimension when one sees it. We draw specific conclusions from the commentaries of some exemplary educators in our lives. Finally, the first four Resources provide detailed staff development activities that can promote and implement the Humane Dimension's four components, and the last two Resources present information on an overview of the Adventure Education Center in Columbus, Ohio, and a generic process of procedures for win/win negotiations, respectively.

At the end of each chapter, we provide a short list of reflective questions on incorporating the Humane Dimension into your work. You may want to jot down your responses for later review and to keep a record of your ideas as they occur while you read. We hope the Humane Dimension will find its way into your own practice and give guidance on enhancing the important work of school leadership.

CORWIN PRESS

The Corwin Press logo—a raven striding across an open book—represents the union of courage and learning. Corwin Press is committed to improving education for all learners by publishing books and other professional development resources for those serving the field of K–12 education. By providing practical, hands-on materials, Corwin Press continues to carry out the promise of its motto: **"Helping Educators Do Their Work Better."**

Acknowledgments

Many of our friends and colleagues should be thanked here, one by one, name by name, but they are too numerous to list. We name only one individually, our graphics specialist and secretary, Sue Kunar. We do want to thank the following groups of people: our colleagues and friends, our peer editors and readers, the significant others in our lives, our parents, our children, and God.

Corwin Press gratefully acknowledges the contributions of the following individuals:

Joanne Arhar, Professor
Kent State University
Kent, OH

Bruce Matsui, Professor
School of Educational Studies
Claremont Graduate University
Claremont, CA

Michele Merkle, Principal
York Suburban High School
York, PA

Terry Orr, Associate Professor
Teachers College, Columbia University
New York, NY

Leonard Pellicer, Author, Dean, Professor
School of Education and Organizational Leadership
University of La Verne
La Verne, CA

About the Authors

**Joseph M. Giancola** has been a public school educator for the past 27 years. Four of these years were spent as a secondary school administrator, whereas 18 of these years have been spent as the assistant superintendent in two different Ohio school districts. After graduating from Kent State University with a bachelor's degree in music education, his studies resulted in certificates to teach music, mathematics, and business in secondary schools. After receiving his Master of Arts degree in Music, he continued his studies in the doctoral program at Kent State's College of Education, where he was awarded the degree of Doctor of Philosophy in 1988. For the past 12 years, Joseph has been the Assistant Superintendent of the Kent City School District in Kent, Ohio. In addition, Joseph is an adjunct professor of Educational Administration at Kent State.

Joseph has coauthored numerous journal articles on educational administration. Along with coauthors Pat E. Crisci and Cynthia A. Miller, he has been published in several issues of the *Government Union Review.* In addition, he and Janice K. Hutchison have been published in the *Ohio ASCD Journal.* His written works and presentations focus on leadership and sharing decisions and power with educators to contribute to school transformation and reform.

The Giancola family consists of Joseph and his wife, Helen, and their three children, Katie, Jerry, and Annie, whose leadership qualities continue to emerge in their high school and college careers.

 **Janice K. Hutchison** has been a classroom teacher for the past 29 years. After graduating from Ohio University with a degree in secondary math, English, and reading, she taught reading for five years in a state institution for incarcerated young men. For the past 25 years, Janice has taught reading and English at Theodore Roosevelt High School in Kent, Ohio, while earning advanced degrees in Education Foundations and Curriculum and Instruction at Kent State University, where she was awarded the degree of Doctor of Philosophy in 1997. Janice now serves as the Coordinator of Staff Development for Kent City Schools and teaches English classes at the high school and graduate classes in Curriculum and Instruction at Kent State.

Janice has coauthored the past two editions of *Dynamics of Effective Secondary Teaching*. She also contributed a chapter, "Maxine Greene and the Current/Future Democratization of Curriculum," in William Pinar's (Ed.) *The Passionate Mind of Maxine Greene*. Her written work and presentations tend to focus on power relations in school reform and classroom democracy.

The Hutchison family consists of Janice and her two children, Cassidy and Mitch, who genuinely explore the alternative conception of *power with* others in their lives.

1

Introduction to the Humane Dimension

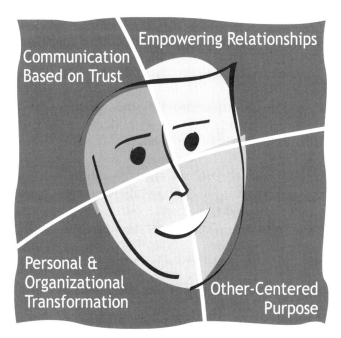

Communication Based on Trust

Empowering Relationships

Personal & Organizational Transformation

Other-Centered Purpose

Humane Dimension

In the workplace, all of us need a language of moral discourse that permits discussions of ethical and spiritual issues, connecting them to images of leadership.

—L. G. Bolman and T. E. Deal, *Leading With Soul* (1995)

BACKGROUND

Portrait of a Teacher

Leslie Leonard had been an English teacher at Theodore Roosevelt High School (Roosevelt High School) in Kent, Ohio, since 1967. Her service there was interrupted by several breaks to raise her family and to participate in a national antinuclear movement and a local child advocacy program. From her first year on the job, Leslie was recognized by her peers as one of those individuals who led by serving. She was one of those teachers who continued to change as she challenged and, inevitably, changed the school around her.

The changes Leslie enacted stood out among her peers and her students because they eventually became embedded in the school culture. For example, in 1995, Leslie initiated community service projects in the Service-Learning Seminar course that she developed. Rather than becoming a stand-alone project, community service eventually became a vital component of several school programs and courses. This gradual development resulted mainly because Leslie did not allow her own ego to become entangled with her professional activities. She patiently nurtured community service with a small group of students within each class. She collaborated with administrators, fellow teachers, and community members by actively seeking their input and consistently inviting their involvement. In return, her work was met with support and encouragement generously provided by her colleagues. After a few years of fostering limited community service projects, Leslie sought out feedback from faculty and students. She admitted, sometimes reluctantly, the flaws in the various service activities and took steps to strengthen the program. Part of improving the student projects required expanding the school/community collaboration aspect of the Service-Learning Seminar beyond the course itself. Other classes, and therefore other teachers and students, became involved. For example, the Home Remodeling class began to work with the local Habitat for Humanity program. Students in a family and consumer studies program initiated partnerships with local child advocacy programs.

Two years earlier, had Leslie attempted to work in isolation, community service would have been relegated to a small group of seniors in a single class. If Leslie had not been willing to admit to the weaknesses in the initial program, other teachers may not have been inclined to participate.

And if Leslie had felt more passionate about the idea of community service per se and less compassionate for her fellow educators and students, the Service-Learning Seminar may have been just another reform effort with limited impact at Roosevelt High School, pursued in isolation.

Since 1995, the community service projects that Leslie began have slowly grown in number and scope. The collaborative environment of personal relationships and trust in which Leslie thrived has been a key factor in the growth of her project and other professional endeavors like hers.

Portrait of an Administrator

From the very beginning, Leslie was supported by the type of school administrator who could distinguish the use of *power over* people from *power with* people. The high school principal, Judy Kirman, saw the potential in Leslie's beginning plans for the Service-Learning Seminar. Judy also knew that the plan could fall apart if critical components like curriculum design, school/community partnerships, and department collaboration were not thoughtfully considered.

Instead of imposing a list of requirements on Leslie, Judy posed a series of questions:

- What do we know about successful student community service programs?
- What have the faculty advisors of those successful programs learned about what works and what doesn't work when students become involved in community service?
- How can one department in a high school initiate student service without limiting the enrollment in other departments' elective courses?
- How will the curriculum of this course be aligned with academic content standards?
- How will this course be evaluated?
- With whom will you share your successes and failures?

Judy did not pose these questions as challenges to be overcome. She posed them as opportunities for personal and professional reflection. Judy encouraged Leslie to ask other faculty and community members to respond to her questions. Judy also gave Leslie two valuable gifts: time (i.e., to reflect, to visit other schools, to write curriculum, and to work with other teachers) and trust (i.e., that empowered Leslie to soar beyond anyone's expectation of her project's potential for success). After the Service-Learning Seminar was initiated, Judy's support continued. She took care to keep lines of communication open between administrators of her team and guidance counselors to reduce scheduling conflicts. Knowing that the increased collaboration between the school and the community could lead to some serious public relations issues, Judy served as the liaison between the high school and the central office. Furthermore, Judy continued her role as Leslie's critical friend by asking even harder questions:

- How can the academic rigor of this program be strengthened without compromising student time in the community?
- Can you describe ways the program can enhance collaboration within the school?
- What lessons can the seminar students teach to our middle school and elementary school students about compassion and service?
- Why do you want to continue building this program?

Responding to these questions was not another item on Leslie's checklist of things to do. She took her time and discussed the questions with her students and with other teachers. Naturally, there were those adults in the building who began avoiding Leslie because they did not feel it was their responsibility to take on her burden. Many of her peers, however, felt it was their "response-ability" to consider the implications of this newly designed course. Not only were they interested in the community service aspect of it and the potential for cross-curriculum projects, but they shared Leslie's compassion for all students. Furthermore, their relationships with each other and with Leslie formed a bond of support. In a recent round of interviews with the entire professional staff, the teachers and administrators at Roosevelt High School described their school as "a place where students can excel in multiple ways" in a culture of positive relationships between and among students, teachers, parents, and administrators.

Landscape of the School

Throughout its history, Roosevelt High School in Kent, Ohio, has maintained a strong reputation of excellence. The school's ongoing commitment to changing and improving has engaged its staff of more than 110 professional educators and student body of approximately 1,300 students in countless successes related to academics, athletics, activities, and the arts over many decades. The school culture of which we speak has been sustained over time and cyclical changes in personnel (viz., teachers and administrators). Its first banner of excellence was hung in its modern auditorium during the 1984–1985 school year. It was during this year that the school was recognized by the U.S. Department of Education with the prestigious Excellence in Education award.

A critical phase in the high school's development came in 1994 when it joined a cadre of buildings in the state of Ohio known as Venture Capital Schools. Funded by the Ohio Department of Education, the venture capital phase lasted five years and earned the school $125,000 in grant funds. The schoolwide initiatives that resulted from this reform effort included the formation of a School Improving Team (SIT). This group of teachers and administrators examined the school practices existing at the time, researched reform literature, and formed a number of meaningful collaborations with Kent State University and the elementary and middle schools in the district. Those five years of collaboration and study planted seeds of significant, long-term change in the school. Along with the many curriculum and instructional changes that resulted from the venture capital was the legacy of the SIT. This group forged professional and personal bonds through summer retreats, weekend brainstorming sessions, and after-school planning meetings. Team members who still work at the high school often refer to that time when personal transformation flourished.

Since the beginning of the 2003–2004 school year, the Roosevelt High School staff has embarked on a new journey of self-reflection in an effort to improve. Teachers and administrators there have agreed to use the process of appreciative inquiry (Cooperrider & Whitney, 1999) to evaluate their past and to decide their future direction. Over a three-month period, in a series of focus groups, the faculty at Roosevelt High School was asked this question: "How would you describe the ideal Roosevelt graduate?" Their responses boiled down to four major attributes. The ideal Roosevelt graduate possessed strong intellectual skills, positive character traits, practical life skills, and effective interpersonal skills. After these skills and traits were defined and illustrated, faculty, students, and parents were interviewed with the appreciative inquiry process.

Appreciative inquiry is an approach to social and institutional change designed by David Cooperrider and Diana Whitney (1999). Here are its two major premises:

1. *Human systems grow toward what they persistently ask questions about . . .*

2. The single most important action a group can take to liberate the human spirit and consciously construct a better future is to *make the positive change core the common and explicit property of all.* (p. 10, italics originally used by authors)

The 115 faculty members, 650 students, and 40 parents who were interviewed answered questions about intellectual skills, character traits, life skills, and interpersonal skills. Each interview encouraged the interviewees to describe "what gives intellectual life, character life, etc. to Roosevelt High School" (i.e., appreciation of the culture), and "what else might be possible in the area of intellectual skills, life skills, etc." (i.e., vision of the culture). An analysis of the 800-plus interview responses revealed some interesting commonalities:

- Students at Roosevelt High School feel genuinely cared for by the adults in the building.
- Relationships between students and faculty and among faculty members are of primary importance.

- There is a sense of authentic community in the building. Students and parents trust the teachers and administrators. Faculty members, for the most part, trust each other and, as a result, are often willing to take curricular and instructional risks.
- Open communication, as characterized by an ongoing, even exchange of information, is a key element of past projects in which risks were involved.

Moving On

On February 20, 2004, Leslie left work early, feeling ill, and was tragically killed in a traffic accident. Three days later, more than 1,000 people lined up at Leslie's church to pay their respects at her calling hours. Hundreds of students stood by with their former and current teachers. Judy Kirman waited in the long line that wrapped around the old stone church. That evening, we expressed our sympathy and our gratitude for Leslie's presence in our lives.

It was at the church service and a school memorial service where Leslie's legacy became clear to anyone who was unsure about what she accomplished. What she accomplished was to touch thousands of individual lives; equally as memorable was how she brought people together. It was almost as though Leslie's primary goal was to ensure that all of her friends, acquaintances, and loved ones would be connected somehow. Divisions between people were not possible under her influence. She personified Roosevelt's professional family as much as Roosevelt embodied her individual spirit.

This book explores what it is about this school and the people in the school that allowed Leslie to flourish both personally and professionally for the past 37 years. We include data from our past 18 years of work and recent results from the appreciative inquiry process (Cooperrider & Whitney, 1999).

THE HUMANE DIMENSION AT WORK

We admit that we are proposing only a small piece of a complex puzzle to improve public education. Any K–12 practitioner, higher education scholar, or national expert already has suggested many theories and effective practices that could support positive change in public education. Discussion of our Humane Dimension does not rule out their work or refute it.

Our work does add one piece to this puzzle, however, which we believe has not been addressed in enough detail to assist school districts in a process of organizational transformation. This piece, our thesis, is the *Humane Dimension—a place in an organization where personal transformation is allowed to occur in a culture of compassion, trust, empowering relationships, and common purposes.* Specifically, we describe a pathway to personal transformation so that, ultimately, organizational transformation may occur and endure. We believe that without this contextual piece, individuals and the organization at large struggle to commit to change that is lasting.

We are not alone in our recommendation to lead for personal transformation. Bolman and Deal (1997) allude to this recommendation when they provide four frames or "lenses" through which individuals interpret and assess situations. Of the four lenses (viz., human resource frame, structural frame, political frame, and symbolic frame), two lenses, the human resource frame and symbolic frame, are similar to our Humane Dimension. That is, the human resource frame emphasizes people's needs and the importance of caring and trusting; the symbolic frame focuses on meaning, symbols, and stories of faith and hope.

We emphasize that this book is about school *transformation,* not school reform or restructuring. This distinction is based on our belief that school reform and restructuring are organizational phenomena, whereas school transformation implies that personal change and transformation precede organizational transformation. Therefore, this book is a handbook on human development, not organizational development. It is a manual on molding trust, relationships, other-centered purpose, and, ultimately, personal transformation within each and every individual of an organization. We argue that though *compassion* and *trust* are common, trite terms in the English language, they are far from having that status in most organizations in which we have worked or studied.

Inputs and Outputs

Most works that focus on improving practices in leadership and teaching and learning typically are based on the inputs or outputs of public education. The inputs encompass a host of variables related to student learning and achievement, whereas outputs (e.g., improved student achievement) are the expectations that emerge from society's political processes such as legislation, judicial reviews, and executive orders.

Yet in this book, we ask the education community to consider the place *between* the inputs and the outputs. We have adapted Easton's model of a political system (as cited in King, Swanson, & Sweetland, 2003) to show the potential impact of the Humane Dimension (see Figure 1.1). We define the Humane Dimension as a place where personal transformation is allowed to occur. In this place, levels of power within an organization are connected by compassion and trust, and people are united by relationships based on common purposes. This dimension is a place where interactions connect the inputs provided by the education community to outputs expected by society.

Figure 1.1   Easton's Model of a Political System Adapted for the Education
System

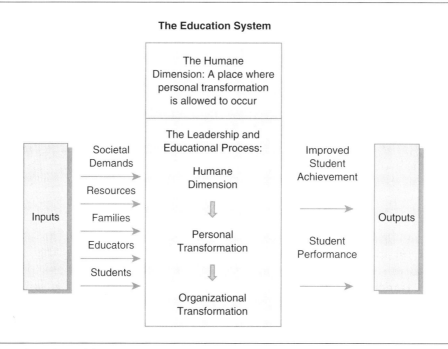

SOURCE: Adapted from King, Swanson, & Sweetland, 2003.

We address a question that a critic might ask: How does the Humane
Dimension improve student achievement? We respond to our critic indirectly. That is, a teacher may have direct, positive impact on student
achievement, but if a teacher's personal and professional needs are overlooked by the organization, this impact might be constrained by barriers
that can limit teacher creativity, flexibility, motivation to change, and
desire to engage in organizational goals. Without such teacher qualities,
the likelihood of lasting change, school reform, or restructuring is
decreased, if not totally denied.

The Potential Gap Between Teachers and Administrators

We believe that there exists the potential for a gap between teachers
and administrators and the risk of creating silos in schools when the components of the Humane Dimension are not present. Evidence of this poten-
tiality may be detectable wherever these two different levels of power and
authority interact. Hall (1995) introduces the notion of a "gap" between
levels of constituents in his work on policy makers and practitioners; he
elaborates that the gap exists in perspectives, semantics, and scope of
work. Furthermore, we also believe that gaps are possible between other

levels of power in the organization; we expand our meaning here to include any employee groups whose authority and power may differ by contract, by law, or even by status in the organization.

Our studies (Giancola, 1988; Hutchison, 1997) in six public school districts in the Midwest generally have identified the existence of multiple cultures or levels of power among teachers, administrators, and other employee groups. In a way, these levels exist on separate, parallel planes that never touch each other.

Evidence of these cultural differences essentially resides in how conversations change when any two of these groups come together. Consider how the conversation may change in the teachers' lunchroom on a day when a district office administrator eats lunch with the staff. No one is saying here that some degree of cordiality, collegiality, and decorum is not present. In fact, these social measures may even appear to be slightly elevated to accommodate the mingling of these two levels of power. The fully truthful conversation, however, may occur after that district office administrator exits the lunchroom. We all have heard it as teachers. Even administrators, who once were teachers of course, can recall readily the kinds of things that were said at the lunch table when they were teachers. These things could include many issues: family, last night's ball game, particular students and families, particular administrators, recent decisions by the district administrators or building principal, and so on.

Other important and equally unfortunate evidence resides in situations that we call "caucus." A caucus occurs whenever a group isolates itself, intentionally or unintentionally, to address an issue without the other group present. Consensus building is impossible under these conditions where all persons are not "at the table" to present their points of view. Obviously, what results is a compromising environment. In this environment, each group or level of power ultimately comes together in conditions where each side has prepared a separate proposal or solution to solve the problem. What is likely to occur is a compromise in which each side gives up a little to find some middle ground.

Senge (1990) implicitly concurs that this potential for a cultural gap exists with his principle of "personal mastery" (p. 139). Senge seeks a commitment to truth in an organization, and he views omission as a lack of truth. He uses the example of a business meeting where what is being thought by the participants is not what is being said. Consider the previous example of a caucus. Each one of us has witnessed situations at meetings or in other forms of communication where individuals withhold, omit, or possibly distort information to accomplish some ulterior goal motivated by a purpose that is not shared by both parties to a decision.

Argyris (2001) also views omission as a lack of complete truth in the organization. He identifies two types of learning: single-loop and double-loop. The former occurs when a simple answer is given to a simple question, but the latter occurs when a second, follow-up question probes more deeply into the respondent's feelings about unspoken issues related to the question. Omission occurs when leaders do not probe more deeply (i.e., double-loop) into issues.

A final evidence and specific example of a caucus is the principals' meeting. Every school has such meetings. At such events, district administrators and building principals plan and share information about district activities. What is problematic here is the nature of the embellishing conversations that occur. Like the previous example of the teachers' lounge, the truthful conversations occur without the other party present. Things said could include issues such as abilities or behaviors of certain teachers, plans to implement an activity or project without input from the personnel who ultimately may be responsible to implement such plans, details of implementation that include a careful withholding (temporarily) or omitting (permanently) of information that might have been useful to other personnel, and others.

Because of differences between groups and possible gaps between levels of power within an organization, a better way is needed to communicate with each other. And so, we next look to the cycle of components that we call the Humane Dimension.

The Cyclical Nature of the Humane Dimension

So many phenomena in physical science, earth science, life science, and even social science are based on cycles. For example, consider in physical science the importance of the cycle of water's transformation from a liquid (i.e., oceans, lakes, and streams) to a gas and back to water in the form of rain. In earth science, consider the cycle of the earth's rotation on its axis and the regular change from night to day. In life science, consider the cycle of a seed (e.g., an acorn) transforming itself into a seedling, a sapling, a fully grown oak tree, and ultimately another acorn.

The most important examples for the purpose of our discussion, however, occur in social science. Consider Bloom's (1956) *Taxonomy of Educational Objectives*. Bloom theorizes that students learn a discipline's concepts at different levels of understanding. A student may progress through a mere knowledge level of learning to a deeper comprehension. Beyond comprehension, a student may be able to apply, analyze, synthesize, and evaluate knowledge. Complete mastery of a concept occurs when a student can demonstrate his or her learning at these varying levels of understanding. When faced with a new concept in that discipline, the student recycles this process of learning, which begins at the knowledge level. Beyond knowledge, the student seeks to comprehend, apply, analyze, and so on to demonstrate mastery of the new concept. Although Bloom did not refer to his taxonomy specifically as a cycle, we espouse that the nature of learning is cyclical as in the previously described process. That is, a learner recycles all or part of this model whenever he or she encounters a new concept. In the course of a school day, week, month, or year, this cycle may be repeated literally hundreds and thousands of times.

Another important example but not as theoretical as Bloom's (1956) taxonomy is the forming of a friendship. When one meets a new friend, one may invest a limited amount of **Trust** in the new **Relationship.** If one is gratified by the first encounter, one may invest a bit more Trust in the second encounter and deepen the Relationship. Increasingly, one's focus becomes more **Other-Centered** and less self-centered. Each meeting may result in a **Personal Transformation** of more **Trust,** deeper feelings, a stronger and more **Empowering Relationship,** and more focus on an **Other-Centered Purpose.** This cycle is almost as though one has an implicit character rubric in mind that evaluates each new level of Trust, Empowering Relationship, and Other-Centered Purpose when a new interaction occurs.

As primitive and simplistic as this example may seem, it is the basis for humans' encounters with each other. We say that **Communication Based on Trust** leads to **Empowering Relationships,** which in turn lead to an increased focus on the other person, or what we call an **Other-Centered Purpose.** Finally, these three components of relationship building lead to a **Personal Transformation** where "the new you" is ready for another encounter with that other person, at which time the cycle starts again. Figure 1.2 graphically depicts this simple notion.

In his *Complex Responsive Processes in Organizations,* Stacey (2001) makes a significant contribution to our cyclical design. He states,

> Individuals in interaction with each other together create the levels of organization and society, and those collective levels constitute the context within which individuals act. In other words, individuals construct organizational/social levels, which then act back to affect those individuals. (pp. 14–15)

Furthermore, in his own "Figure 2.1, Mainstream Thinking: The System of Learning and Knowledge Creation" (p. 16), he captures a substantively similar concept of a recursive cycle of interactions, although his focus is not on Trust, Empowering Relationships, Other-Centered Purpose, and Personal Transformation.

Weick (1995) also makes a significant contribution to our cyclical design in Figure 1.2. In his *Sensemaking in Organizations,* he states,

> Sensemaking is about the enlargement of small cues. It is a search for contexts within which small details fit together and make sense. It is people interacting to flesh out hunches. It is a continuous alternation between particulars and explanations, with each cycle giving added form and substance to the other. (p. 133)

Figure 1.2   The Humane Dimension: A Cycle of Components in
                  Transformation

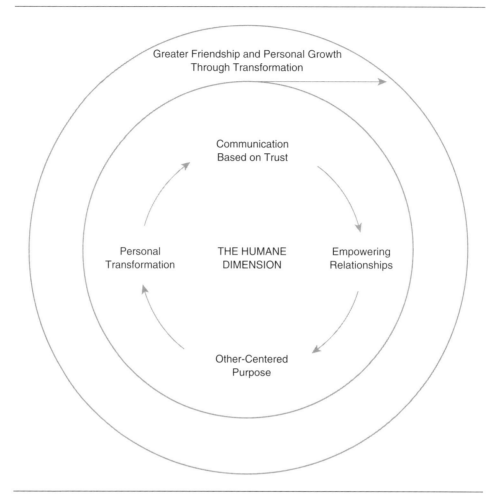

Greater Friendship and Personal Growth
Through Transformation

Communication
Based on Trust

Personal
Transformation

THE HUMANE
DIMENSION

Empowering
Relationships

Other-Centered
Purpose

Each of the previous authors therefore recognizes the importance of a recursive cycle of interactions that build on previous interactions. In short, their work confirms for us what we have observed at Roosevelt High School in Kent and other schools.

The growth of a friendship, then, is depicted by an increasing number of layers (i.e., concentric circles) of **Personal Transformation.** This cycle is the essence of the Humane Dimension. In this dimension, Personal Transformation is allowed to occur time after time in a culture of compassion—compassion between and among all levels of members in the organization. **Empowering Relationships** sprout up in an atmosphere of **Trust** that allows individuals to experience the empowering freedom to grow as human beings, friends, and colleagues of other people.

So, we believe that the body of an organization's employees transforms itself one person at a time. The focus of school leaders, then, must be to support **Personal Transformation** on a one-on-one basis. Levels of formal power must be connected by compassion, Trust, Empowering Relationships, Other-Centered Purpose, and Personal Transformation.

INTEGRATING ROUTINE MANAGEMENT (I.E., THE MANAGERIAL DOMAIN) AND THE HUMANE DIMENSION

We believe that all too often there is an emphasis on managing, but not managing *and* leading organizations. Before we discuss this very important balancing act, let's take a closer look at each set of behaviors. Kotter (1996) makes the distinction between these two different types of leadership behavior when he states,

> Management is a set of processes that can keep a complicated system of people and technology running smoothly. The most import aspects of management include planning, budgeting, organizing, staffing, controlling, and problem solving. Leadership is a set of processes that creates organizations in the first place or adapts them to significantly changing circumstances. Leadership defines what the future should look like, aligns people with that vision, and inspires them to make it happen despite the obstacles. (p. 25)

Another way of making this distinction is to look at the day-to-day activities of any organization and to imagine how things could be different. We offer contrasting ideas within the framework of our Humane Dimension in Figure 1.3. We note that the day-to-day activities are those routine things that must occur daily for the organizational policies and procedures to be carried out. What should underpin these policies and procedures, then, are organizational goals.

We acknowledge and emphasize that many routine or day-to-day activities are necessary realities for school leaders. We say that these activities exist in the Managerial Domain of leading, a necessary dimension where managerial activities must be carried out. Both Fayol (1949) and Sears (1950) have identified classical elements of management: planning, organizing, directing, coordinating, and controlling. (We do not wish here to associate any negative meaning to the Managerial Domain. In fact, there are many cases of school governance that must be carried out in the Managerial Domain.)

Consider the example of employee unions, where certain types of communications, such as explanations, may be required by law during interim periods between contract beginning and ending dates, in lieu of reopening

Figure 1.3   Identifying the Managerial Domain and the Humane Dimension

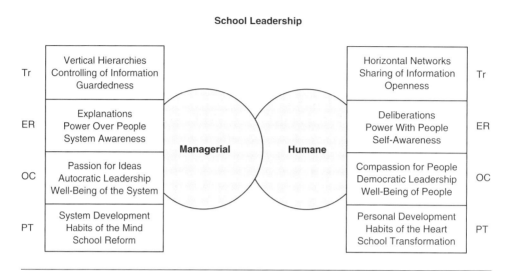

NOTE: Tr = Trust; ER = Empowering Relationships; OC = Other-Centered; PT = Personal Transformation

authentic deliberations. Also, state laws often define *power over* within the context of administrative contracts but not teacher contracts. Our use of a dichotomy in Figure 1.3 is simply to unravel, not to undermine the routine, day-to-day operations of a school.

The challenge for any leader, then, is to enhance the role of manager and elevate his or her thinking, wondering, and aspiring to a higher level. Kotter (1996) asks administrators to lead, not just manage. We ask them to move between the Managerial Domain and the Humane Dimension whenever possible.

Consider Figure 1.3's dichotomies related to the Humane Dimension's first component of relationship building, namely, Communication Based on Trust. The manager emphasizes sustaining vertical hierarchies, controlling information, and maintaining guardedness in communications. We suggest that to be a leader, one must *also* emphasize horizontal networks between and among levels of power, share information, and create openness in communication. Successful school leaders balance these roles, avoiding the gravitational pull to be a manager *or* a leader.

In relationships of the Managerial Domain, the manager relies on explanations, position power over people, and system awareness or adherence to organizational policies and procedures. In contrast, in the Humane Dimension's second component, namely, Empowering Relationships, the leader emphasizes the importance of group deliberations, power shared with people, and self-awareness. Combining the managerial domain with its humanistic counterpart evidences a holistic approach, effective in both managing and maintaining strong shared leadership.

In the day-to-day, routine activities of the Managerial Domain, the manager demonstrates passion for ideas, believes in autocratic leadership, and protects the well-being of the system. In the Humane Dimension's third component, namely, Other-Centered Purpose, the leader shows compassion for people, believes in democratic leadership, and protects the well-being of people. Still, when these two domains intersect, amazing things can happen. They are not mutually exclusive.

Finally, in the Managerial Domain, the manager emphasizes development of the system, promotes habits of the mind, and espouses school reform. In the Humane Dimension's fourth component, namely, Personal and Organizational Transformation, the leader emphasizes personal development, promotes habits of the heart, and espouses school transformation over reform or restructuring. Throughout the book, we offer practical applications for managers to avoid being trapped in the day-to-day activities of the Managerial Domain and to support making room for increased emphasis on the compassionate components of the Humane Dimension. Although day-to-day, managerial activities are a part of an organization's operation, these activities are not sufficient for an organization to succeed and accomplish lasting change in the long run.

Transformation's Capacity to Connect
Potential Gaps Between Two Cultures

Our studies have shown that both Personal Transformation and Organizational Transformation have the capacity to connect the potential gap between levels of power between teachers and administrators and to fuse the mission and connection between teachers and principals. For example, consider the case of Leslie Leonard's growing and thriving at Roosevelt High School, described at the beginning of this chapter. Getting to **Personal Transformation,** however, is a slow process of developing **Communication Based on Trust, Empowering Relationships,** and **Other-Centered Purpose** in an organization.

Like the cycle of the acorn's transformation into a magnificent oak tree, the cycle of the Humane Dimension takes time. In the self-similar pattern of individuals' Personal Transformations, the larger, similar pattern of Organizational Transformation may undergo many years of taking root. From the many seeds of Personal Transformation, that is, individual-by-individual or one-at-a-time, Organizational Transformation blossoms with no clear end. Just as each spring the oak tree becomes larger, stronger, and more beautiful, Organizational Transformation can grow even when members of the organization think it is as good as it can be.

At Roosevelt High School, we have observed a culture of successful Organizational Transformation that has grown and lasted for the past

40 years under several different leaders. This example is evidence that many Personal Transformations can sustain the Organizational Transformation as different leaders come and go.

As the circle of Organizational Transformation grows, its outer edges reach the parallel planes of the teachers' and administrators' culture. This growth forms a lasting connection, as it were, between teachers and administrators. In Figure 1.4, we conceptually depict this growth and ultimate connection with layers of concentric circles.

Different from the acorn-and-oak-tree example given previously, a deep and lasting human relationship is our final example of this cycle leading to Personal Transformation. We cite a man and a woman who are celebrating their fiftieth wedding anniversary. According to the U.S. Census Bureau (2002), "Five percent of married couples in 1996 had been married 50 years or more" (p. 9). This low percentage is some indication of the challenge of longevity (i.e., longevity of physical health, emotional health, and a lasting relationship) in not only marriage but also in long-term Personal Transformations. Over the past 50 years, this man and woman have been through many changes, emotional, physical, and other-wise. They probably have endured the range of possibilities from success to hardship, happiness to sorrow, and good health to ill health. Through each tribulation, they have experienced Personal Transformation that may have been unprecedented. But with each Transformation, there occurred an increase of Trust, a deepening of their Empowering Relationship, and a greater Other-Centered Purpose. One can only imagine how many of such events could occur during 50 years of marriage.

Yet, through a large series of Personal Transformations, the two people have emerged over and over again as one, a unified embodiment of trust and love, a married couple who have endured life's greatest and worst events. And now, as of their fiftieth anniversary, this man and woman have transformed their union into something far different from what it was 50 years ago. This event describes a transformation of the union, not just of the individuals involved.

Thus, in the present tense, one can only imagine what the transformed organization might look like in, say, 50 years. So, from the many seeds of Personal Transformation, that is, individual-by-individual or one-at-a-time, Organizational Transformation blossoms with no clear end. Just as each spring the oak tree becomes larger, stronger, and more beautiful, Organiza-tional Transformation can grow even when members of the organization think it is as good as it can be. It is only a coincidence of nature here that the oak tree does not produce acorns for its first 50 years of growth. This coinci-dence of nature, however, suggests to us that some cycles take time and that deeply rooted Organizational Transformation is the same way.

In the next four chapters, we present each of the four components in the Humane Dimension's cycle. Definitions are linked to recommenda-tions for action by way of specific staff development activities.

Figure 1.4   Transformation's Capacity to Connect Potential Gap Between Two
Cultures

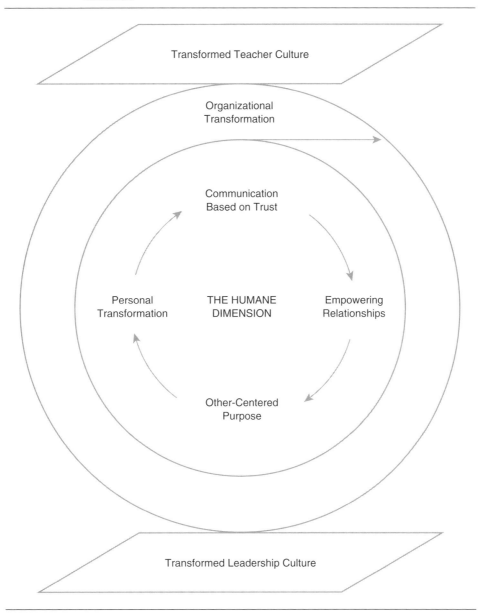

APPLYING THE HUMANE DIMENSION

Specific staff development activities are provided for each of the four components of the Humane Dimension in the Professional Development
Notepad exercises (see Resources A, B, C, and D). Here we remind you of

the components and process of achieving the Humane Dimension, namely, the following:

- Communication Based on Trust
- Empowering Relationships
- Other-Centered Purpose
- Personal and Organizational Transformation

REFLECTION

Q: Based on what you know about the Humane Dimension and thinking in your own school setting, where are there moments or evidence of the Humane Dimension?

Q: Where would you like to see more effort toward achieving the Humane Dimension?

Q: What are some ideas that you have to start this important work?

2

Humane Dimension Component 1

Communication Based on Trust

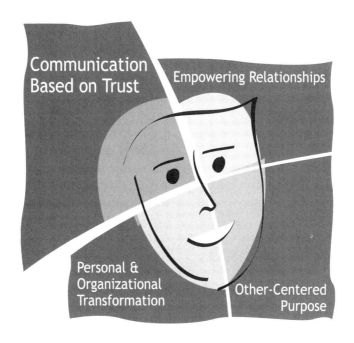

A new moral principle is emerging, which holds that the only authority deserving one's allegiance is that which is freely and knowingly granted by the leader in response to, and in proportion to, the clearly evident servant stature of the leader. Those who choose to follow this principle will not casually accept the authority of existing institutions. Rather, they will freely respond only to individuals who are chosen as leaders because they are proven and trusted as servants. (pp. 23–24)

—R. K. Greenleaf, *Servant Leadership* (1977)

During the final case study of Roosevelt High School from 1994 to the present, our observations of professional development activities, initially generated by the five-year Venture Capital Grant, enabled us to assess the staff's renewed commitment to personal growth and to each other. The natural flow of events during this time of change confirmed our conclusion about the importance of **Trust** in the cycle of the Humane Dimension.

In the material that follows, we include some of the many responses that were made by the Roosevelt professional staff during focus groups that we conducted on the Humane Dimension. These responses are documented in many pages of notes and are presented throughout the next six chapters under the heading of Focus Group Response.

Trust, the beginning of the cycle in the Humane Dimension, cannot be assumed. If it were an everyday occurrence among all individuals of an organization, the conversations between workers would change at all levels of the organization. Unfortunately, the reader may determine how rare is the trust of which we speak in every nook and cranny of an organization.

If Trust cannot be assumed in an organizational culture, then the question is begged: What is Trust? In addition, we ask: How can it be developed in individuals and in the organization such that Personal Transformation can occur? To respond, we look to our observations and some research on trust and make recommendations for practical application.

Guided by the literature (Autry, 2002; Avolio & Bass, 2002; Collins, 2001; Giancola, 1988; Greenleaf, 1977; Hord, 1995; Hord, Rutherford, Huling-Austin, & Hall, 1987; Hutchison, 1997; Jourard, 1971; MacGregor, 1960; Motley, 2004; Sergiovanni, 1994; Sizer, 1992; Wood, 1992) and experience from our studies at Roosevelt High School and five other Midwest public school districts, we have identified four of Trust's simplest, yet distinct, definitions (*Merriam-Webster*, 2004):

- To rely on others
- To have faith in someone
- To confide in someone
- To expect confidently from others

Each of these four actions of Trust is corroborated in the references that follow.

TRUST MEANS TO RELY ON OTHERS

To trust someone means to rely on someone, just as a sick person relies on a doctor or as an invalid relies on a caretaker or servant. Greenleaf's (1977) earliest writing on servant-leadership recounts the story of a servant named Leo. In this story by Hesse (1956), Leo is the central figure who accompanies a band of men on a mythical journey. Leo sustains these men with his menial chores, his spirit, and his song. At some point in the journey, Leo disappears. One of the party, the story's narrator, discovers Leo years later. The narrator finds that, in fact, Leo is the titular head, the great and noble leader of the order that sponsored the journey years ago.

In this story, Leo eventually was granted authority by his order when the members who were led freely and knowingly granted him the power to lead. That is, his order freely responded to Leo's servant stature by choosing him to lead, because he first was proven and trusted as a servant on whom others *relied.*

Greenleaf (1977) speaks often of the importance of Trust developed by the servant as leader—also known as servant-leader—within an organizational community. He states that the servant-leader must elicit Trust "because those who follow are asked to accept the risk along with the leader" (Greenleaf, 1977, p. 30).

Thus, to trust a leader is to rely on the leader and to accept risks along with the leader. One relies on another because he or she respects the other's justice and integrity. One is willing to follow the leader because he or she first had been served by this leader. This simple formula is not unlike the Golden Rule. That is, the essence of the Golden Rule in a leadership context might be:

Lead others as you want to be led.

> **Focus Group Response**
>
> "Sergiovanni (1992) discusses the concept of substitutes for leadership, which differs from participatory leadership and shared leadership. We do things because they are right. This challenges the notion that only administrators can serve as instructional leaders when teachers are in the position to do so."

This ethic of reciprocity in the Golden Rule is found in many cultures. Concise and general, this simple principle is the basis for Hesse's (1956) story of Leo and Greenleaf's (1977) work on the servant-leader. Greenleaf's (1977) presumption that organizational members will follow the leader because they first had been served by this leader is more likely to happen as a result of this ethic of reciprocity.

A final example of relying on someone occurs in Sizer's (1992) work about a fictional, composite character named Horace. An experienced teacher, Horace knows that his school's routines virtually guarantee inadequate work from his students; thus, Sizer's book title is *Horace's Compromise.* But Sizer says, "Horace is to be trusted [i.e., relied on]—trusted to know what is best for kids, what kids need to flourish in the world— and Franklin High's immediate community is to be trusted to know what standards are or might be" (p. xii). We believe that Trust is a necessary precondition to implementing the standards and curriculum that the state and the local community require.

In our Professional Development Notepad examples (see Resource A), we refer often to the Adventure Education Center, an outdoor facility designed for staff retreats and team building. This center's primary focuses are building trust, improving communication, and enhancing collaboration. Weick (1995) recognizes the importance of these kinds of trust-building activities when he states, "If people want to share meaning, then they need to talk about their shared experience in close proximity to its occurrence. . . . This may be why outdoor education retreats seem to be successful means to build teams" (p. 188).

TRUST MEANS TO HAVE FAITH IN SOMEONE

To trust someone means to have faith in someone, just as members of a mountain-climbing expedition have faith in and are connected to the experienced and skilled leader who stakes the ridge so others can ascend safely. Avolio and Bass's (2002) work on transformational leadership compares having faith in someone to having inspired motivation. In fact, they identify one of four components of transformational leadership as "inspirational motivation" (Avolio & Bass, 2002, p. 2).

Consider a leader who motivates others by delegating responsibilities on the basis of individuals' interests and needs. The leader here is inspiring by providing meaning to the work assigned his or her followers. Such assignments based on interests and needs do not mean that duties are not connected to organizational goals. Rather, assignments are made within the context of organizational goals. Avolio and Bass (2002) affirm that followers want to meet expectations of their leader and accomplish goals of the organization when they have faith in their leader. At the same time that their needs and interests are being met, the organization is moving forward because of the accomplishment of shared goals.

The key to integrating individuals' needs and interests with organizational goals is through a process of sharing a vision of the future and ways to get there. Avolio and Bass (2002) state, "The follower needs to feel valued by the leader, the follower needs to find meaning in what he or she is doing, and the follower needs a sense of ownership in what's being done" (p. 6).

Sergiovanni's work (1992) on *Moral Leadership* is akin to this notion of intrinsic motivation based on shared values. In his discussion of a covenant of values documented by a school building's staff, he notes that what is rewarding gets done (i.e., intrinsic motivation), and what is good gets done (i.e., moral-based motivation evolving from a sense of duty).

Ownership of organizational goals results from all members sharing in the vision and direction toward which the organization is moving. Sharing a vision or covenant results from the trust and team connectedness that underpin the process and conversations that occur to develop these organizational goals. What is important here is that trust and team connectedness form the foundation of a shared vision; this foundation generally is formed as a result of thoughtfulness, hard work, day-to-day commitments to each other, and actions, not just words. Such process and conversations eschew implications that there exists some magical phrase or vision statement that, in and of itself, has the capacity to change or guide an organization's path or to shape individuals' behaviors.

In addition to Trust and team connectedness, humility must be an element in the process of developing a shared vision and having faith in others. Humility means "taking the first step at dropping pretense, defenses, and duplicity. It means an end to 'playing it cool'" (Jourard, 1971, p. 133). This element requires that members participate in the process without assuming that the final outcomes will represent all of their own desires and expectations. Instead, all members must be prepared to offer their own ideas and to search for commonalities between individuals' ideas

> **Focus Group Response**
>
> "When I think of practicing humility, first I apply it to my classroom. This means that we know what we are saying has importance in an authentic way."

and the group's collective consensus. Ultimately, a shared decision, goal, or vision is one in which individual ideas integrate through a process of consensus building. (We examine consensus building after completing our discussion of humility.)

In *Good to Great*, Collins (2001) addresses the need for humility in leaders. The leaders and companies of his studies have the commonality of excellent results under the leadership of individuals who understand the balance between ambition and humility. He states that the "Level 5 Executive [i.e., the highest rating of a leader] builds enduring greatness through a paradoxical blend of personal humility and professional will" (p. 20). Later, Collins purports that a great leader "channels ambition into the company, not the self" (p. 36); this action is an act of humility. Similarly, and to create more of what we call the Humane Dimension, Collins emphasizes recruiting and keeping employees who share this profile. See Chapter 6 on building a team and recruiting the right personnel.

Follett's (1924) work on consensus building emphasizes the creative experience of sharing in a decision. She views any conflict or dispute as an opportunity to create a new solution through the process of integration or consensus building. Follett posits that opinions of people involved in group decision making are shaped by the process itself. Specifically, each person involved in the process influences the thinking of others, so that the final product or decision is not merely the sum of the individual contributions but rather something new and different from that sum; that is, some degree of Personal Transformation will have occurred. Thus, the final decision is a new and creative solution—an integration—resulting from consensus, not compromise. She notes that with compromise, participants give up pieces of their viewpoints to move the decision along; this is not the case with consensus.

> **Focus Group Response**
>
> "When I think of 'Communication Based on Trust,' I think about day-to-day interactions, not a speech or a memo. Approachability is key here and so are decency, personal warmth, and regard for the whole person."

Later in this book, we discuss in depth the importance of the team's development as a prerequisite for having faith in one another and creating a shared vision. We defer the remainder of this discussion to Chapter 6, in the section "Team First/Vision Later."

TRUST MEANS TO CONFIDE IN SOMEONE

To trust someone means to confide in someone, just as a friend shares feelings and life's events with another close friend in an atmosphere of safety and security or as an employee shares with his or her supervisor the facts of a situation that might be threatening to the welfare of the organization. Jourard (1971) discusses at length the consequences and benefits of confiding in others, which he calls "self-disclosure" (p. 3). These benefits occur when an individual chooses the road of openness in an atmosphere of Trust rather than concealment in one of distrust, misunderstanding, and even alienation.

Two relatively neutral consequences of self-disclosure are identified by Jourard (1971). First, individuals discover their similarities and differences in such areas as their "thoughts, feelings, hopes, and reactions" (p. 5) to phenomena from their present and past experiences. Second, an individual learns about another's needs; this experience enables the first to help the second or vice versa.

Four benefits of confiding in others are discussed by Jourard (1971). First, he states that "Being heard and touched by another who 'cares' seem to reinforce identity" (p. 87). Second, confiding in others mobilizes spirit. Third, the prior two benefits promote self-healing.

The fourth benefit of confiding in others indirectly alludes to an earlier discussion on humility and its relationship to having faith in another. Jourard (1971) states:

> Authentic being means being oneself, honestly, in one's relations with his fellows. It means taking the first step at dropping pretense, defenses, and duplicity. It means an end to "playing it cool," an end to using one's behavior as a gambit designed to disarm the other fellow, to get him to reveal himself *before* you disclose yourself to him. (p. 133)

Jourard (1971) finds "a correlation between what persons were willing to disclose to other people in their life and what these other people had disclosed to them" (p. 13). In short, he discovers a reciprocity or mutual disclosure in self-disclosure. This discovery is not unlike an earlier discussion on having faith in others and the Golden Rule.

Another interesting discovery of Jourard (1971) is gender-related. He states in his research of the literature that men "tend more to relate to other people on an I-It basis than women" (Jourard, 1971, p. 36). In other words, male leaders tend to create a psychological distance between them and their individual followers; in addition, they tend to avoid obtaining overly intimate or personal knowledge about their followers' feelings and needs.

Probably Jourard's (1971) most important finding in relation to our definition of Trust in the Humane Dimension is that "disclosure of one's experience is most likely when the other person is perceived as a trustworthy person of good will" (p. 65). Another way of stating this finding is that people will tell someone almost anything if they think a person can be trusted and wants to listen to them. Jourard likens this phenomenon to "a secret society" (p. 67) springing into being.

TRUST MEANS TO EXPECT CONFIDENTLY FROM OTHERS

To trust someone means to expect confidently from others, just as ministers, priests, or rabbis confidently expect goodness and kindness from members of their congregation or as benevolent parents confidently expect the best behavior from their children. This type of expectation is captured well by Collins (2001), who states, "The tone of the school should explicitly and self-consciously stress the values of unanxious expectation ('I won't threaten you, but I expect much of you'), [and] of trust" (p. 208).

Stated differently, to trust someone is to expect the truth from someone. This definition of trust is reinforced by Autry (2002) in his work on char-acteristics of servant-leaders. He states that leaders who are trusting do not try to control people; rather, they focus on caring for others and being a useful resource for followers. They confidently expect that their followers will work best in conditions where their needs and interests are being met while, at the same time, they are accomplishing organizational goals. Such leaders view their role in a support capacity; they view themselves as a resource for others.

> **Focus Group Response**
>
> "If I'm feeling valued, I sense the freedom to try new ideas. My opinions are asked and my program and my students are supported. People listen, and they show that they care."

MacGregor (1960) believed that a leader's ability to Trust and expect confidently was related to his or her beliefs about human beings. He theo-rized that two contradictory views of human behavior exist. One view is described as Theory X, and the other is described as Theory Y. Although his theory is somewhat dated, its logic continues to offer some explanation for two different kinds of actions taken by leaders more than 40 years later.

Theory X assumptions about human behavior are likely to underpin an autocratic style of leadership. This leader would not trust followers enough to delegate authority and responsibility on the basis of individu-als' needs and interests. This leader is likely to focus on compliance and might use methods of intimidation and force to get results. A Theory X leader relies heavily on the authority vested in him or her by the organi-zation and by virtue of his or her position in the hierarchy. His or her focus is likely to be one of organizational policies, procedures, internal and external regulations, laws (i.e., local, state, and federal), and judicial deci-sions that impact the organization.

Theory Y assumptions about human behavior are likely to underpin a democratic style of leadership. This leader would collaborate with followers to share in decision making about the organization's vision and goals. This leader wants to facilitate and support efforts made by followers to achieve organizational goals. A Theory Y leader focuses on a follower's self-control and self-discipline; he or she also believes that employees want to have own-ership in their jobs and want to do the best job possible. A Theory Y leader is interested in the Personal Transformation of each follower by focusing on a follower's self-initiative. As Sergiovanni (1992) states it in *Moral Leadership,* the focus is on doing the right thing (not just doing things right).

In her powerful analysis of every wave of school reform since 1982, Hord (1995) concludes that "Effective leaders regularly and frequently check on the implementers to solicit needs and inquire 'how things are going.' This action is two-fold: Implementers feel valued and cared for, and a clear signal is given that the change is of high priority and deserves attention" (pp. 98–99). We view that Hord is recognizing the partial benefits of integrating both Theory X and Theory Y beliefs. Her attention to a balance between feeling valued and cared for and checking regularly and frequently on implementers demonstrates an integration of Theories X and Y. In an earlier work, Hord et al. (1987) also demonstrate a balance between compliance and regulation (i.e., Theory X) and implementers' self-discipline, independence,

> ### Focus Group Response
>
> "Professional respect should be present from the very start of a relationship. Professional respect is evidenced when an administrator trusts that the teacher knows her job and her subjects. . . . If not trusted, many teachers tend to retreat. . . ."

and ownership in their own work (i.e., Theory Y).

In Wood's (1992) *Schools That Work,* there is another implicit example of Theory Y. At Central Park East Secondary School (CPESS), Principal Deborah Meier focuses on two goals that make the success of CPESS possible: "a sense of community that is built here, and a narrowed yet richer curriculum" (p. 43). Further, at CPESS, Meier's efforts to empower teachers and students to be successful were clear in democratic strategies such as eliminating the "huge and impersonal" environment of large city high schools, creating smaller "houses" as organizational centers for students, and implementing the concept of student advisory, "a group arrangement in which one adult develops a relationship with a number of students" (p. 44).

More evidence that MacGregor's (1960) Theories X and Y still have some validity and impact in public schools can be found in Georgia. "Top-down mandates that attempt to control everything from what children learn to how teachers teach" (Wood, 1992, p. 58) are clear examples of Theory X, mandated at one time by Georgia Quality Basic Education (QBE). In reaction to QBE, Eliot Wigginton's project of empowering his high school English classes at Rabun County High School in Clayton, Georgia, is a clear example of his students' capacity to publish the *Foxfire* magazine, an ongoing school literary work.

Another characteristic of servant-leaders identified by Autry (2002) is that they focus on building a community at work. Extensive study on this characteristic has been done by Sergiovanni (1994). Building a community where members care about each other and make a total commitment to each other is another way of describing Trust as expecting confidently from others. In such a community, members—that is, both leaders and followers—confidently expect each other to support any work that advances both the profession and the goals of the organization.

Sergiovanni (1994) describes many forms of community where Trust implicitly is a part of the commitment made by its members and where individuals confidently expect each other's best work. Like MacGregor's (1960) Theory X and Theory Y, Sergiovanni's (1994) forms of community contrast two contradictory views. One is *Gemeinschaft,* which Sergiovanni describes as "the bonding together of people that results from their mutual binding to a common goal, shared set of values, and shared conception of being" (p. 6); further, he states that "*Gemeinschaft* exists when connections within and among people are based primarily on loyalties, purposes, and sentiments" (p. 57).

In contrast to *Gemeinschaft, Gesellschaft* is said to exist "when connections within and among people are based primarily on the rational pursuit of self-interest" (Sergiovanni, 1994, p. 57). The former term assumes a view of human behavior that is similar to Theory Y, whereas the latter term assumes a view of human behavior that is similar to Theory X (MacGregor, 1960).

Another characteristic of servant-leaders identified by Autry (2002) is that they do not hold on to territory; they let go of their egos. Servant-leaders are more prone to decentralize because they trust and confidently expect followers to succeed to a greater extent because of their degree of autonomy. Greenleaf (1977) states that leaders "are learning to decentralize in a way that creates a variety of environments in which different styles of able people will flourish and be themselves" (p. 157). He also sees decentralization as a first step in accommodating the wide differences and needs of members in an organization.

The purpose of servant-leaders is not to manage but to lead by becoming a resource and supporting the efforts of followers. Greenleaf (1977) states that "the new ethic requires that *growth* of those who do the work is the primary aim, and the workers then see to it that the customer is served and that the ink on the bottom line is black. It is *their* game . . ." (p. 158).

A final characteristic of servant-leaders identified by Autry (2002) is that they create a place where people can do good work and find meaning in their work. Leaders who trust and confidently expect excellence from their staff delegate responsibility on the basis of individuals' needs and interests. This type of leader understands his or her role in helping others to grow by accommodating followers' wishes where practical. When asked what business a leader is in, he or she responds: "*I am in the business of growing people*—people who are stronger, healthier, more autonomous, more self-reliant, more competent" (Greenleaf, 1977, p. 159).

> **Focus Group Response**
>
> "This is about building relationships over time. Trust is a factor."

In summary, we have defined Trust, the first component of the Humane Dimension, in terms of four actions:

- To rely on others
- To have faith in someone
- To confide in someone
- To expect confidently from others

IMPLICATIONS FOR PRACTICE

Suggestions From Practitioners on Communication Based on Trust

Just as the Humane Dimension is a cycle of relationship-building components, so is the cycle of organizational transformation a process of culture-building steps. Practitioners from our focus groups have suggested the following model to promote Communication Based on Trust.

Planting the Seeds (Today) . . . The Acorn

A principal new to Our Town Elementary School announces at his first staff meeting of the year that the teachers will develop on their own the agenda for the monthly staff meetings in the upcoming first semester. Furthermore, with the teachers' permission, the principal will not attend these meetings. Rather, he will meet afterward with the group's leader to ask the question on all agenda items: "How can I help and support you with your goal?" Subsequent to these staff meetings, the teachers begin to see evidence that the principal's main goal is to help and support them. Meanwhile, the teachers notice that day-to-day, mundane announcements are handled through brief memos rather than afterschool meetings called by the principal.

Searching for First Results (Short-Term) . . . The Seedling

By the beginning of the second semester, the Our Town Elementary teachers request that the new principal begin to attend the monthly staff meetings. These teachers continue to develop on their own the agenda for such meetings, but they wish to eliminate the extra step of the group leader's meeting with the principal. Of course, the principal agrees to attend future staff meetings at the request of the teachers.

Looking for Growth (Intermediate-Term) . . . The Sapling

By the beginning of the second year of this principal's tenure at Our Town Elementary School, the teachers ask the principal to contribute his own agenda items to their monthly staff meetings. Of course, the principal agrees to attend staff meetings *and* to contribute his own agenda items. This principal focuses on professional discussions pertinent to changes in curriculum and assessment recommended or mandated by the state's department of education.

Transforming the Culture (Long-Term) . . . The Oak Tree

By the beginning of the third year of this principal's tenure at Our Town Elementary School, the teachers not only ask the principal to continue contributing his own agenda items to their monthly staff meetings, but they also ask for his input on how to address and change many other aspects of the building's programs, to include operations, curriculum and instruction, assessment, and other areas. Of course, the principal agrees to attend staff meetings *and* to contribute his own agenda items *and* to offer his input on how to address and change many other aspects of the building's programs. This principal focuses not only on professional discussions pertinent to changes in curriculum and assessment recommended or mandated by the state's department of education but also on professional discussions about many other aspects of the building's programs.

APPLYING THE HUMANE DIMENSION

Specific staff development activities for building Trust are provided in the Professional Development Notepad exercises of Resource A.

REFLECTION

The following reflective questions about Trust should be answered before moving on to the next chapter.

Q: Based on what you know about Trust and its four definitions, think about your own school setting. Where are there moments or evidence of Trust?

Q: Where would you like to see more effort toward achieving Trust?

Q: What are some ideas that you have to *start* this important work?

Q: What strategies might teachers try to *cultivate and sustain* Communication Based on Trust?

Q: What strategies might building principals and district administrators try to *cultivate and sustain* Communication Based on Trust?

Q: In what ways can *you* help now to *initiate and cultivate* Communication Based on Trust in *your* building culture? In your district culture?

3

Humane Dimension
Component 2

Empowering Relationships

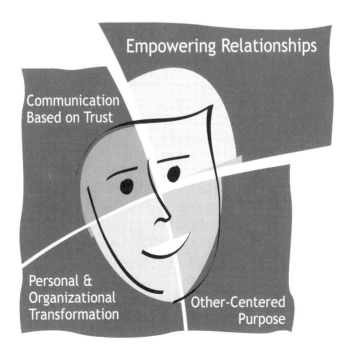

> *Schools will remain intractable to desired reform as long as we avoid*
> *confronting (among other things) their existing power relationships.*
> *. . . Avoiding those relationships is precisely what educational reformers*
> *have done, thus ensuring that the more things change, the more they will*
> *remain the same.*
>
> —S. Sarason, *The Predictable Failure of Educational Reform* (1990)

Empowering Relationships are the second step of the Humane Dimension's cycle and can have the most positive impact of all four components in the cycle. To understand this step, we first review the conventional paradigm of power and control in organizational relationships, and then we suggest an alternative. A major issue related to empowerment in school reform, according to Sarason (1990), Hutchison (1997), and Popkewitz (1991), is the existence of traditionally hierarchical relations in schools. Conventional hierarchies often can delay the development of Trust and the restructuring of power that must be shared through professional relationships. What is it about conventional hierarchies and power relations in schools that can delay or even constrain reform? A look into the career of just one teacher can illustrate what "existing power relationships" (Sarason) can do to even the most genuine attempts to change.

TRADITIONAL CONCEPTIONS OF POWER IN SCHOOLS

Part of Leslie Leonard's story was discussed earlier. She was involved in a reform initiative at her high school. The initiative was a service-learning project integrated with a humanities curriculum. A yearlong study of Leslie's reform work (Hutchison, 1997) focused on the teacher's perceptions of institutional supports and barriers to her efforts. Although her work on this project was considered successful, Leslie revealed some interesting findings, through a series of interviews and journal entries, about power relations in schools.

Leslie began teaching in the late 1960s. In her first year of teaching, she recalled being "encouraged, supported, and assisted in developing a team-taught course that met the needs of students in the late '60s. Experimentation, exploration and cooperation were expected and rewarded. I didn't know this was the exception to most teaching experience" (Hutchison, 1997, p. 150). After teaching for another ten years, Leslie left the classroom to devote her time and energy to community volunteer work.

On her return to public education about eight years later, Leslie saw a need for a program that integrated leadership training, contemporary reading/writing development, and character education through volunteerism in the community. The superintendent and Leslie's department chair supported the initial stage of exploration, and the seminar's pilot semester began in January 1996. A year later Leslie realized that, in her naiveté, she "did not follow the appropriate channels and did not inform the right people in the right order." That is, the layers of power in the district's organization began to block her progress in this initiative, even though she had clearance from the highest level of power in the school district, the superintendent.

Leslie compared her recent reform efforts to the initiative she undertook 30 years earlier when she "developed the experimental team-taught course and had a carte blanche from the administration. I trusted myself, and I expected that trust to be reflected through the process I chose" (Hutchison, 1997, p. 151). Leslie's recent work was often deterred by a complex and not easily identifiable "chain of command" (p. 152). As she reflected on her reform work, Leslie concluded that "understanding the underlying power issues may be more important than I realized to planning for success" (p. 152).

A summary of Leslie's journal entries and interviews (Hutchison, 1997) generally reveals how traditional power relations can negatively affect reform work in schools:

- *Bureaucratic Structures.* Leslie describes how the vision of her seminar had been "bridled and tamed" by traditional school practices of funding, staffing, and scheduling.
- *Lack of Trust.* Leslie felt distrusted when her recommendations for student numbers, makeup, and schedule were disregarded. This disregard made her doubt herself.
- *Handling of Information.* Leslie found that the way information was handled within the school system assured that "people in power control the power." She experienced many instances when information was not shared openly. In one journal entry, Leslie wrote:

    If true creative initiatives are to thrive, there must be an atmosphere of Trust where those in charge give away the need to always know more or to have total information about all that is going on. In order for those in power to be totally informed, a cumbersome, unwieldy process unfolds that demands triplicate reports, committee meetings, long deliberations, hearings, and other processes that either greatly hamper the progress of the project or stop it altogether.

- *Traditional Models of School Leadership.* Leslie saw the "conventional views" of educational leadership as a serious constraint to her reform work. To achieve one of the few leadership roles in a school,

many educators have to undergo a series of steps. By the time they
reach positions of power, they may or may not be willing to "be
open and honest about power." What is perpetuated by this mode
of developing school leadership is a traditional view of power relations. It is that view, according to Leslie, that helped make education
"so bulky and awkward and traditional that it doesn't respond easily at all. . . . It sort of moans and groans when you kick it and then
lays back down and sleeps" (Hutchison, 1997, p. 165).

What Leslie described in these reflections is the cumbersome reality
of traditional power relations in many schools. Words like "empowerment"
and "power" began as part of education reform slogans and have evolved
into an "inherited tradition" (Wittgenstein in Cherryholmes, 1988) that
remains, for the most part, unexamined. Sarason (1990) addressed this concern in his book, *The Predictable Failure of Educational Reform: Can We Change
Course Before It's Too Late?* His main contention is that current efforts at
school reform will fail unless existing structures of power within schools
are reviewed and restructured. We agree with Sarason on this point.

What schools need to reduce their innate intractability, according to
Sarason (1990), is a close examination of their existing power relationships.
Many current proposals for school reform ignore his point that

> the classroom and the school and school system generally are not
> comprehensible unless you flush out the power relationships that
> inform and control the behavior of everyone in these settings.
> Ignore these relationships, leave unexamined their rationale, and
> the existing "system" will defeat efforts at reform. (p. 7)

The reviewing and restructuring of power relations in schools prove
problematic mainly because of two dominant traits of the school setting.
The first trait has to do with understanding of parts versus understanding
of systems; the second trait has to do with unexamined professional roles
that sometimes seem to conflict with one another.

Understanding of Parts Versus Understanding of Systems

According to McCutcheon (1995), most school personnel employ
"flawed linearity" in their thinking and perceptions about schooling and,
therefore, have difficulty understanding the school as a system. McCutcheon
cites Senge (1990) in contending that "we learn best from experience, but
[in an organization] we never directly experience the consequences of
our most important decisions" (as cited in McCutcheon, 1995, p. 155). The
"flawed linearity" that marks most educators' thinking and perceptions
stems from a narrow understanding of the work of schools. Sarason (1990)
believes that many educators lack a

sophisticated conception of schools as systems. Teachers, principals, curriculum specialists, superintendents, members of the board of education—with rare exception, those who belong to these groups think and perceive in terms of parts and not a complicated system: *their* parts, *their* tasks, *their* problems, *their* power or lack of it. (p. 24, emphasis in original)

What accompanies this partial understanding of the system is a partial vision of goals. Often, "turfism," that is, territoriality, can preclude principals and teachers from totally open communication. Each of us who works in a school district has at one time in our career withheld information to further our project. We have, at times, not held up our end of an assignment because the objective was not one of our own. We have been part of the force that separates a school system into disconnected components like the following:

- Elementary schools and secondary schools
- Administrators and teachers
- Gifted education and regular education
- Resource room staff and inclusion staff
- District office administrators and building administrators

The system is fraying apart, and even a rallying cry like "We want what is best for students" can mean different things to different players.

Unexamined Professional Roles

The second trait of schools that makes the changing of traditional power relationships problematic, according to Sarason (1990), is that unexamined professional roles sometimes seem to conflict because of adversarial stances. Sarason sees a direct connection between this trait and the understanding-of-parts trait. He notes that each school group—principals, teachers, curriculum specialists, and others—

knows that there is a "system" by which each sees it from a particular perspective which, by its narrowness, precludes understanding of any other perspective. One might expect, for example, that those in administrative positions, each of whom had occupied lower-level positions (as teachers), would in their recommendations indicate a sensitivity to and comprehension of those below them—that is, one would expect a discernible degree of overlap in their perspectives. This is rarely the case. Predictably, they see themselves as adversaries. (p. 7)

We tend to address these conflicts in our schools in a variety of ways. Some people simply ignore them. Others acknowledge their conflicting professional roles and relations at school as "just one of those things" and try to tiptoe around them. After a frustrating meeting in which our own ideas are blocked, perhaps because of these stances, it can feel pretty good to engage in a little (or a lot of) complaining. Eventually, we can find ourselves blocking, too.

As long as we educators refuse to move beyond our confining perceptions about the roles and relations in schools (i.e., understanding of parts) and continue to ignore the conflicting professional roles that may exist in a school setting, we will limit our involvement to activities in the Managerial Domain because the Humane Dimension will be stifled. It is evident from Leslie's narrative as well as from educational reform research that ignoring power relationships in schools prevents us from building Trust. Yet what other options do we have when it comes to power and empowerment in our schools? How else can we construe power relationships? What will it take to get us there? The answer is an alternative paradigm.

AN ALTERNATIVE CONCEPTION OF POWER IN SCHOOLS

One of the most thorough studies of power and empowerment in education was completed by Kreisberg in 1992. Kreisberg's work, *Transforming Power: Domination, Empowerment, and Education,* contrasts a predominant conception of power with an alternative conception. The predominant image and interpretation of power in our culture and, hence, our schools, is what Kreisberg calls *power over,* defined as "a conception of power as the ability to impose one's will on others as the means toward fulfilling one's desired goals. It is the ability to direct and control and to manipulate and coerce if need be, sometimes for the good of all, most often for the good of the few" (p. 45).

In schools, we experience traditional *power over* in the Managerial Domain when Trust is not openly shared in our communications with others. Information becomes a commodity and is used to buy power. Decisions are made, for example, about a districtwide budget with limited information shared between principals and teachers. Committees of principals and teachers make textbook selection recommendations and later learn that their recommendations have been modified or superseded. Faculty meetings are used to disseminate pieces of information. Professional evaluations are designed as hoop-jumping activities rather than as formative professional growth. *Power over* is evident when the real purpose of a project is to serve the needs of selected individuals who may have the power at that moment. Perhaps public relations about the project will further these individuals' agenda. (Of course, we are not implying that all principals or teachers engage in this type of behavior when they have a leadership role.)

Kreisberg (1992) was concerned that a definition of power as domination limited human capacity in schools and, as a result, offered an alternative conception of power in schools, one that he called *power with*—what we associate with Empowering Relationships. Included in Kreisberg's review of the literature on *power with* are the works of Fromm (1947), May (1972), Miller (1976), and Surrey (1987). Fromm claimed that people must be free of domination to develop to full capacity, and that it is only within the context of relation with others that an individual can realize power. May described *power over* as exploitative power but *power with* as integrative power. Miller extended Fromm's argument about individual transformation when she wrote, "In a basic sense, the greater the development of each individual, the more able, more effective and less needy of limiting or restricting others she or he will be" (p. 116). In other words, the more one is capable of *power with,* the less one will seek *power over.* Surrey equated *power with* as power together, power emerging from interaction, power in connection, relational power, and mutual power. She also linked *power with* and empowerment through her contention that empowerment is nurtured through *power with relationships.* According to Kreisberg, the earliest and clearest distinction between *power over* and *power with* was made by Follett (1918, 1924, 1941). Follett believed that power "conferred" is doomed to failure and that *power with* "is not a zero-sum proposition where one person gains the capacity to achieve his or her desires at the expense of others" (Kreisberg, 1992, p. 71).

From his summary of theories about power, Kreisberg (1992) identified these key concepts of *power with:* interpersonal dynamics, reciprocal influence, emergence, relationship, coagency, sharing, giving, and openness. *Empowerment, then, is "the ability to make a difference, to participate in decision making, and to take action for change.* Empowerment does not assume control of resisting others, but emerges from work with others who are also deciding, acting, and making a difference" (p. xi). However, Blanchard, Carlos, and Randolph (1996) use a simpler approach to defining empowerment when they state: "People already have power through their knowledge and motivation. Empowerment is letting this power out" (p. 20).

IMPLICATIONS FOR AN ALTERNATIVE CONCEPTION OF POWER

For schools to move from traditional stances of *power over* to more humane approaches of *power with,* or Empowering Relationships, educators must be willing to examine how they talk with each other, how they perceive personal development, how they view leadership roles, how they structure schools, and why they do what they do at work.

Group Deliberations

The nature of group deliberations within schools—when they are not truly two-way communication—has been characterized in some cases by teachers' references to poor communication, conflict, ambiguity, and a need for order and predictability (Hutchison, 1997, p. 200). The need for order and predictability, according to Wheatley (1992) and Glasser (1990), diminishes human potential and openness within an organization. Instead of this *need for order,* perhaps what is called for in schools is a *creation of order,* which, as Wheatley writes, can occur

> when we invite conflict and contradiction to rise to the surface, when we search them out, even support people in the hunt for unsettling or disconfirming information and provide them with the resources of time, colleagues, and opportunities for processing the information. (p. 116)

Instead of avoiding conflict related to power, then, what we could be doing is developing a critical awareness about it in the very specific sense of investigating how power relations are affecting specific school programs. In short, if we are deliberate about restructuring control and power relations, we could achieve Empowering Relationships in the Humane Dimension's cycle.

Mezirow's (2000) work on "learning to think like an adult" includes a relevant comment on our society's understanding of discourse as debate. Mezirow (2000) cites Tannen's referral to our society as an "argument culture" that "conditions us to approach anything we need to accomplish together as a fight between opposing sides, like a debate or like settling differences by litigation" (p. 11). Our purpose for discourse is "to win an argument rather than to understand different ways of thinking and different frames of references, and to search for common ground, to resolve differences, *and to get things done"* (p. 12, emphasis added).

In schools, the quality of our discourses is compromised because, often, we limit our goal to winning an argument. We have overlooked the greater purpose of discourse. Kegan (2000) contends that the two most powerful yearnings of all humans are to be included and to have a sense of agency. "Of course," Mezirow (2000) writes, "agency is intimately dependent on others and on one's inclusion in discourse. Discourse always reflects wider patterns of relationship and power" (p. 11).

Issues of Adult Ways of Knowing

The research on adult ways of knowing (Belenky, Clinchy, Goldberger, & Tarule, 1986; Kegan, 1994; Mezirow, 2000) argues that adults learn under certain conditions and in ways that differ from children and adolescents.

Minstrell's (1999) study of tacit knowledge in teaching concludes with recommendations for professional expertise through informal observations, reflections, mentoring, and active participation in professional networks. The previous section on "Group Deliberations" made clear that it is in ever expanding patterns of relationship and power that adults develop, learn, and transform. It is in these patterns of behavior that the Humane Dimension recursively cycles through its components. The conditions for free and full participation in adult learning, and thus Empowering Relationships in the school, include:

- Access to . . . accurate and complete information.
- Openness to alternative points of view: empathy and concern about how others think and feel.
- The ability to weigh evidence and assess arguments objectively.
- Greater awareness of the context of ideas and, more critically, reflectiveness of assumptions, including their own.
- An equal opportunity to participate in the various roles of discourse (Mezirow, 2000, pp. 13–14).

Along with meeting these conditions for adult learning and empowerment, principals and teachers who facilitate staff development must be aware of two kinds of learning. Informative learning brings about changes in *what* we know. Transformative learning brings about changes in *how* we know (Kegan, 2000, p. 54). Informational and transformational kinds of learning are each valuable and important activities. Each can make a difference in our schools.

Traditional staff development offers opportunities for informative learning. But in order for individual educators and, consequently, schools, to be transformed, other, transformational kinds of learning must take place. Imagine inservices like the following:

- Individual teachers are given time to read literature on a topic like assessment or teaching writing. These teachers are encouraged to write their questions and concerns, and then, in small groups, engage in deliberations about their reflections.
- Faculty members on a grade-level team or in a department openly share their assumptions about why they teach a specific topic in specific ways. These assumptions are challenged in a safe, caring environment.

Notions of Educational Leadership

Educational leadership must be exercised in many forms by teachers, principals, and board office administrators. By equating educational leadership with only administrative roles and no others (Maxcy, 1991), we severely limit our conceptions of leadership and empowerment. The ongoing professional development of teachers and principals should be directly tied to new leadership roles and responsibilities. Clark and Astuto (1994) point out that school administrators are not alone in having and using the knowledge or the experience to be the instructional leaders in schools; both principals and teachers may share such expertise:

> What claims to expertise can they make if they are to be instructional leaders? They began as teachers. How have they now accumulated the expertise to establish school goals, assess curricular decisions, and evaluate teacher performance? Surely such changes have not come about as a consequence of their graduate study. Graduate training for educational leader is one of the few areas in education that has remained impervious to reform over the past 20 years. Yet it is one of the areas most in need of reform. (p. 518)

Thus, graduate programs that integrate curriculum and instruction studies with educational administration studies could do a great deal to expand notions of leadership in schools. Educators who choose to stay in the classroom could then study leadership theories and develop sound leadership practices within their roles as department chairs, team leaders, or grade-level leaders. School principals would be able to integrate their traditional leadership studies with emerging research on teaching and learning. Empowerment could then come to mean more than a "conferring of power." Empowering as "the ability to make a difference" and "to take action for change" (Kreisberg, 1992, p. xi) could become a daily reality for teachers and administrators.

Consider a broader view of leadership and empowerment. Deal and Peterson (1999) suggest that "Everyone should be a leader. . . . It is not only the formal leadership of the principal that sustains and continuously reshapes culture but the leadership of everyone" (p. 87).

A Changed Bureaucratic Structure in Schools

Significant and genuine change in our schools is seriously hampered by the "limited imagination" (Astuto, Clark, Read, McGree, & Fernandez, 1994) that governs how educators view both district and school roles and processes, like the design of the faculty master schedule, student schedules, and task specifications. Time and time again, teachers point to the lack of time and the lack of resources as major constraints to their own reform work. Preconceived notions dictate the following:

- What is an appropriate amount of discretionary time a teacher needs to work effectively?
- What is an appropriate amount of money a teacher needs to purchase instructional resources and professional development?

- What is an appropriate amount of input about program modifications and development a teacher should offer?
- What is an appropriate organizational structure to accommodate and support all of the previously listed?

To become critically aware of these pervasive traditions, or bureaucratic structures, all educators should learn to view the teacher's role beyond the confines of the classroom and the principal's role beyond the limits of conventional management. This kind of view is not likely to take shape unless discretionary time and opportunities for professional collaboration are shared by classroom teachers and principals alike. Of equal importance is, as discussed in the previous section, an enhanced conception of educational leadership. Further inquiry is needed about how discretionary time is made available and is used in other schools outside the United States (e.g., Japanese and German schools).

In addition to limited thinking (i.e., traditional thinking) applied to school processes such as schedules and task specifications are the enduring assumptions applied to administrative bureaucratic structure. The development of an organization's structure must reflect the real interactions and methods of its decision-making processes. Sizer (1992) describes the "hierarchical bureaucracy" (p. 205) of schools as "lumbering" and "stifling" (p. 209). It will take commitment from both principals and teachers to change this "pyramidal governance" of schools.

We turn to the circle as a starting point for discussion of an ideal organizational structure. Consider the example of a strong family where love, truth, and honor are exchanged continually among all members. To encapsulate how these family members make decisions in an organizational chart would be ludicrous; however, it is not difficult to imagine the exchanges of mutual love that drive this family's discussions and decisions. Although the parents traditionally have the final word on most family decisions, it is likely that most conversations leading to a final decision occur in a circle of relationships (see Figure 3.1). Whether

> **Focus Group Response**
>
> "Teachers should be given opportunities (e.g., time, money, support) to try out their own new ideas. [We would] build on people's strengths, not their weaknesses."

through "table talk" of all members or one-on-one interactions between, say, a father and son or mother and daughter, the discussions are more likely to occur in circles of dialogue where, temporarily, all members share a lateral plane of thoughts and contributions. It is true that the parent may sway the final decision, but we ask the reader to consider this rhetorical question: Would a traditional, vertical hierarchy of superiors and subordinates describe the true process used by this family to make a decision? We respond in the negative here, and we reinforce the need for Empowering Relationships in families, schools, and other organizations.

Figure 3.1   A Decision in a Circle of Family Relationships

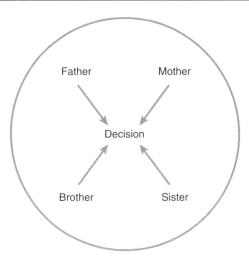

Analogously, we challenge the effectiveness of an organizational chart to describe how decisions are made. Although the traditional chart demonstrates "where the buck stops," it hardly complements the complex web of interactions and methods actually used to arrive at final decisions. Thus, we recommend that a board of education display two charts in its policy book: one to document where the final accountabilities rest and one to document how decisions will be made in the organization and how participants will be empowered. Such documentation would be useful for all stakeholders in defining their roles in decision making and participatory leadership structures. These roles will be discussed in further detail in Chapter 6, "Elements of a Transformed Leadership Culture."

A New Motive Behind Education Reform

The motives that drive reform work in schools too often remain undisclosed. This is not to say that all reform work is motivated by the personal perspectives of a few. However, because discussions about motives rarely occur in group deliberations, what can result is distrust. Open Communication Based on Trust could help establish, *one by one, group by group, then faculty by faculty,* the kind of districtwide setting in which Relationships are Empowered by each other's Other-Centered Purpose. In this kind of environment, Leslie's initiative to change traditional teaching-and-learning arrangements in her high school would be met with support and commitment to empower her.

IMPLICATIONS FOR PRACTICE

Suggestions From Practitioners
on Empowering Relationships

Just as the Humane Dimension is a cycle of relationship-building components, so is the cycle of organizational transformation a process of culture-building steps. Practitioners from our focus groups have suggested the following model to promote Empowering Relationships.

Planting the Seeds (Today) . . . The Acorn

A district's entry-year program ensures that each new teacher is partnered with a mentor teacher throughout the first year of teaching. At the orientation meeting in August, entry-year teachers meet their mentors to discuss questions and concerns about the first few weeks of teaching. To establish a culture of ongoing assistance, each mentor is released from classroom teaching for two half-day sessions each month during the first two months of school. During this time, the mentor/entry-year teacher pairs have the following options.

- The mentor observes the entry-year teacher and gives feedback on the lesson.
- The entry-year teacher observes the mentor, and they discuss the new teacher's questions and insights.
- The mentor teaches the entry-year teacher's class to model specific strategies requested by the new teacher.
- The mentor covers the entry-year teacher's class while the new teacher observes other teachers.
- The mentor and entry-year teacher plan a lesson or unit together.

Searching for First Results (Short-Term) . . . The Seedling

By November, the entry-year teacher and mentor relationship has taken on a coaching quality with feedback and support offered within the context of classroom teaching. The partners begin to explore implications for professional practice outside the classroom as well. One entry-year teacher and her mentor agree to join the building's intervention assistance team. For the rest of the year, they prepare for meetings together, attend the meetings, and afterwards, reflect on the content of each meeting (i.e., what was discussed) and the process of the meetings (i.e., how discussions were carried out).

Not only does the entry-year teacher begin to learn about teacher responsibilities outside of the classroom; she also is advised on teacher leadership behaviors like adult deliberation skills and faculty collaboration.

Looking for Growth (Intermediate-Term) . . . The Sapling

During the second semester, entry-year teachers identify one area of concern about their teaching. These areas of concern become the basis of individual action research projects. Each mentor acts as an entry-year teacher's research advisor, helping the new teacher to select relevant literature and collect and analyze data. For example, one entry-year teacher who teaches physics at the high school is concerned about how few female students participate in class discussions. With her mentor's help, the new teacher reads several articles on gender equity in the science classroom. The mentor observes the new teacher's class once a week for a month and records on a seating chart the number of times students participate in discussions. Together the entry-year teacher and the mentor design two interventions to increase female student engagement, and after implementing these interventions, the mentor again collects participation data. The pre- and postdata are reanalyzed, and the entry-year teacher develops a plan for future action based on their conclusions. By the end of the semester, the new teacher realizes that being empowered to change her teaching has many unforeseen implications for future practice.

Transforming the Culture (Long-Term) . . . The Oak Tree

During the second and third years of teaching, the action research projects from the entry year become the impetus for ongoing professional development. Topics are investigated in greater depth in study groups, graduate courses, workshops, and so on. Second- and third-year teachers become district specialists on a variety of topics like gender equity in the science classroom, designing relevant homework, teaching strategies such as sophisticated note taking, and so on. The expectation is that these teachers will share their information within grade-level, team, or department meetings. The district also publishes a quarterly newsletter, *Teachers Leading Teachers,* with articles by the teacher researchers and announcements for teacher presentations at various buildings in afterschool sessions.

APPLYING THE HUMANE DIMENSION

Specific staff development activities for developing Empowering Relationships are provided in the Professional Development Notepad exercises of Resource B.

REFLECTION

Q: Based on what you know about Empowering Relationships, think about your own school setting. Where are there moments or evidence of empowerment?

Q: Where would you like to see more effort toward achieving Empowering Relationships?

Q: What are some ideas that you have to *start* this important work?

Q: What strategies might teachers try to *cultivate and sustain* Empowering Relationships?

Q: What strategies might building principals and district administrators try to *cultivate and sustain* Empowering Relationships?

Q: In what ways can *you* help now to *initiate and cultivate* Empowering Relationships in *your* building culture? In your district culture?

4

Humane Dimension Component 3

Other–Centered Purpose

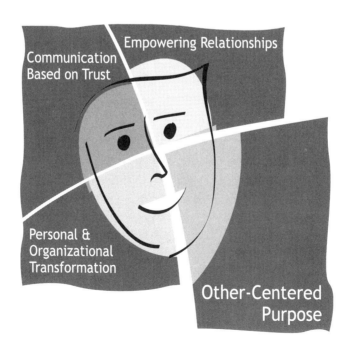

Pressures of immediate tasks and the bottom line often crowd out personal needs that people bring into the workplace. Every organization is a family, whether caring or dysfunctional. Caring begins with knowing about others—it requires listening, understanding, and accepting.

—L. G. Bolman and T. E. Deal, *Leading With Soul* (1995)

An Other-Centered, not self-centered, Purpose is the third step in the Humane Dimension cycle. It grows out of Trust and Empowering Relationships. When an individual trusts and builds an empowering relationship with another, this individual's focus turns almost entirely toward the other person. Consider the young bride and groom on their honeymoon. Each person's focus is almost exclusively on the other person. Such levels of trust, relationship, and other-centeredness are higher, perhaps, than at any other time for these individuals.

An analogous example of Other-Centered Purpose in education might be the new teacher. Observe the beginning of the school year after all the students have been introduced, and the impact of new lesson plans is being measured by this new teacher. Her levels of trust, relationships, and other-centeredness (i.e., student-centeredness) are higher, perhaps, than any other level developed during field experiences and student teaching, which immediately preceded this teacher's first teaching contract and assignment.

Such examples of pristine and unprecedented focus on someone other than the self can be imagined by almost anyone. It is easy to say that these examples are the direct opposites of self-centeredness.

We all should be able to recall one of our favorite teachers. It is likely that such recollection includes an image of a human being whose Other-Centered Purpose is as clear to us today as it was back then. In fact, as we have matured since that impression was formed originally, our perspective of our favorite teacher's Other-Centered Purpose probably has deepened with regard to an enduring understanding of just how much that teacher influenced us. In short, we likely recall the relationship engendered more than the content taught.

Personal relationships such as the bride-and-groom and teacher examples previously mentioned are not the only place in need of Other-Centered Purpose based on Trust and Empowering Relationships. Even though an innumerable amount of relationships will be developed among members of an organization, the relationships between the actual institution and its members also are in need of these components of the Humane Dimension. Next, we elaborate on the institution as servant.

AN ASSESSMENT OF THE CURRENT STATE
OF OTHER-CENTEREDNESS IN ORGANIZATIONS

We briefly turn to Greenleaf's (1977) work on Other-Centered Purpose in the business environment. He boldly starts one of his chapters in a most direct manner: "This is my thesis: caring for persons, the more able and the less able serving each other, is the rock upon which a good society is built" (p. 62). Anyone's critique of this thesis might be: But of course, this is common sense; it is the Golden Rule. Here we dig more deeply to explore the details.

Typically, a business enterprise is viewed as an organization committed to its own balance sheet, profit-and-loss statements, and the "bottom line" (i.e., the final and last number on the balance sheet that indicates how much more revenue than expenses the business earned in one quarter, half, or year). This view could be unfair for business owners who consider themselves servants to their employees, patrons, and other constituents. Greenleaf (1977) elevates everyone's thinking of a business or institution as a *servant* when he espouses that

> the only sound basis for trust is for people to have the solid experience of being *served* by their institutions in a way that builds a society that is more just and more loving, and with greater creative opportunities for all of its people. (p. 83)

We believe along with Greenleaf that institutions that generate a high level of Trust through a quality of service to all ultimately will prevail as the best institutions or businesses with the best bottom line, widest profit margin, and most consistent balance sheets. In the institution as servant, an Other-Centered Purpose as a way of operating is likely to rely on a servant's power of example to persuade instead of a coercive power to dominate and manipulate people.

An example of an institution as servant is Roosevelt High School under the leadership of current building principal Roger Sidoti. His entire focus is the support of teachers in his building. He views his primary role as one of support—moral support for new ideas that are consistent with building and district goals, financial support that funds the resources needed for existing and future projects, curricular and instructional support that helps the teacher to connect new ideas to existing teaching and learning in the building, and creative support that is intended to stretch the teacher into new areas that, perhaps, were not considered. The staff has a great deal of Trust in Roger because of his continuous support. He also tries to attend to as many professional and personal needs of his staff members that he has the capacity to accommodate. The staff members view their building's harmonious Empowering Relationships as a caring family where they know that listening, understanding, and accepting will occur daily. Over time, the relationships have cycled through a deepened sense of appreciation and respect. The staff members have opened their minds and hearts, accepted their own vulnerabilities, and become present for one another. In this building, the staff members have been led with soul and compassion. These observations are well documented in the notes taken during Roosevelt's recent appreciative inquiry (Cooperrider & Whitney, 1999) process.

In other literature on leadership, the essence of Other-Centered Purpose is captured in models that espouse the importance of human relations. Hersey, Blanchard, and Johnson (1996) emphasize the leader's power of relationships with others to engage them in the establishment and accomplishment of organizational goals. Other leadership models that are similar to Hersey et al.'s typically include a balance between relationships-oriented behavior and task-oriented behavior of leaders (Blake & Mouton, 1964; Cardinal, 1985; Hersey et al., 1996; Kotter, 1996; Senge, 1990; Stogdill & Coons, 1957).

> **Focus Group Response**
>
> "High visibility and greater contact with administrators give us teachers the sense that they know what we are doing."

When leaders focus on human relations with others, they find time to listen to others in both one-on-one and group settings. Such leaders understand the importance of listening for the benefit of others and view their roles as resources to others (Hersey et al., 1996).

Conversely, when leaders focus on the task at hand, they are quick to assign particular tasks to individuals or to a group. Such leaders are clear about what the task is, what the expectations are, and what to do after the task is completed (Hersey et al., 1996).

> **Focus Group Response**
>
> "Leaders have to get to know each person's strengths and passions."

When a leader is able to focus on both the relationships with others and the task at hand, the optimal effectiveness in a situation may be achieved (Hersey et al., 1996). Effectiveness, then, is the third dimension of Hersey et al.'s model (i.e., relationships and tasks are the first two dimensions). To these authors, the third dimension of effectiveness, portrayed graphically in their work, is a measure of the balance between relationships and tasks encouraged by organizational leaders.

The concept of a balance between relationships-oriented and task-oriented behaviors of a leader also is espoused by Cardinal (1985) in his work on structured interviews for administrators and other leaders. The interview is comprised of questions that seek candidates' responses, which reasonably compare to a rubric. This rubric is the result of documenting and analyzing the responses of successful administrators and leaders who were interviewed in the past. The basis of the interview is twelve leadership competencies. One of these competencies, *performance expectation*, includes the effectiveness criterion that Hersey et al. (1996) stipulate regarding the balance between relationships and task. Cardinal writes about a hypothetical candidate in his optimal administrative profile: "This person tends to have an excellent understanding of the balance needed between the performer and the performance" (p. 2).

> **Focus Group Response**
>
> "They [i.e., leaders] need to balance a passion for ideas with compassion for people."

In our original focus groups, which we designed to follow up on details of the Humane Dimension, we posed a list of dichotomies that demonstrated the difference between components of the Managerial Domain and the Humane Dimension. Under the category of Other-Centered Purpose, one of the dichotomies emphasized the difference between *institutional behavior* and *intimate behavior*.

In the Managerial Domain, members of the organization treat each other like an institution. Bolman and Deal (1995) state it in another way: "Pressures of immediate tasks and the bottom line often crowd out personal needs that people bring into the workplace" (p. 103). In the Humane Dimension, members of the organization connect their hearts and souls, and daily, they transform their relationships.

> **Focus Group Response**
>
> "Ask me, 'What can I do for you?'"

This transformation is how we defined the term "intimate behavior" in our focus groups. Generally, the response to this and other dichotomies was a repeated phrase stated by both teachers and administrators: *It all comes down to Trust.*

We observed recently an example of *institutional* versus *intimate* behavior in a local fast-food restaurant. While we were eating there, a customer stepped up to the counter to register a complaint about the quality of the special order that he had placed. He complained that the one item that he had requested on the sandwich was too meager of an amount, and he wished to have more of that item put on his sandwich. What he proceeded to do in the remainder of the conversation with the young lady working behind the counter was to destroy her self-image with a litany of belittling comments about the franchise, the general quality of work from today's young people, and her own apparent laziness to allow such an abomination to happen to this customer. Needless to say, this young woman was devastated. She had been treated as though she was an institution, not a person. She was treated as though she herself was some huge, corporate conglomerate that did not care about any aspect of the customer's wishes. Had she been treated with compassion, there might have been a personal connection between herself and the customer; a transformation of both parties might have occurred; or a display of warm and intimate personal behavior might have been exchanged.

Later, in Chapter 6 on the elements of a transformed leadership culture, we emphasize the importance of selecting (i.e., hiring) and building (i.e., developing) a team of employees who bring similar virtues to the organization, to include an emphasis on intimate, not institutional, behavior. A balance between relationships-oriented and task-oriented behaviors will be considered optimal for both employee satisfaction and, at the same time, task (i.e., results that reflect optimal student achievement) accomplishment.

> ### Focus Group Response
>
> "Being visible means building relationships; to be other-centered, you have to get past your own ideas and your own vision. You need to be flexible and fluid. You should use others as a barometer, a gauge."

Before moving on to the next section on the current state of expectations in schools, we challenge our readers to assess their own organizations' capacity to become a servant to the professional and personal needs of others. Responses to the following questions may indicate the need for work on the first three components (i.e., Trust, Empowering Relationships, and Other-Centered Purpose) of the Humane Dimension in the work environment.

Trust

Do organizational leaders have faith in followers to do the right thing with a minimum of supervision?

- In what ways do leaders demonstrate this faith in followers?
- How do followers react to leader's faith to do the right thing?
- Under what conditions should leaders exercise their authority to supervise?

Empowering Relationships

Do members of the organization share power and information through open communications?

- In what ways do the organization's members demonstrate open communication?
- What effect does open communication have on each person's ability to make a difference?
- Under what conditions should power and information not be openly shared?

Other-Centered Purpose

Is there a compassion for people that takes precedence over a passion for ideas and tasks to be performed?

- In what ways do members of the organization demonstrate that a compassion for people takes precedence over a passion for ideas?
- What effects can a compassion for people have on an organization's transformation?
- Under what conditions should the members of an organization decide to emphasize their passion for an idea over compassion for people?

AN ASSESSMENT OF AN EMPHASIS ON RESULTS AND EXPECTATIONS OF PUBLIC SCHOOLS

In education, like business, there are constituents and stakeholders who expect, even demand, results (i.e., quantitative results). The analogy of business profits and students' test scores becomes the mantra of the bottom-line watchers. But even with these stakeholders, the merits of Other-Centeredness and servant leadership (Greenleaf, 1977) must be examined for their long-term implications with respect to practice and results.

We are not naive about the need to study student test scores at the national, state, and local levels. It is not difficult at the national level, however, to damage the public's perception of and confidence in the quality of American schools through the misuse of data. Reflecting on the school reform reports of the early 1980s, DuFour and Eaker (1992) agree: "The education profession was essentially a target of, rather than a participant in, the excellence movement that followed *A Nation at Risk* (Gardner, 1983)" (p. 10).

One national example of test results and public perception was the Third International Mathematics and Science Study (TIMSS) (National Center for Education Statistics, 1997). Although the TIMSS report could have been used constructively in public education to improve curriculum, instruction, and test results in mathematics and science, this study was reported to the American public with an irrevocable thrashing of educators' work and students' efforts that, in actuality, was stretched to sensationalism on the basis of many inaccurate and inequitable comparisons (Bracey, 1997). The public education system's recovery from such misuse of data became the emphasis, then, rather than the accountability intended by the TIMSS designers. Because of public sentiment spurred by such national reports, school districts' purposes have dramatically shifted toward quantitative results and away from Other-Centered relationships.

State testing programs (e.g., state proficiency test, state graduation test, state achievement test, etc.) are a second way to study student achievement. The public's call for accountability may be witnessed through the efforts of state legislatures that mandate such testing programs and state report cards. Results such as these become the focus of almost all educational activity in state school systems, such that reporting results becomes a race for having the highest test scores and state-report-card grades in comparison to other school districts in the immediate surrounding area within reach of the local newspaper. We do recognize, however, each community's concern and desire for improvement of its local school district's test scores and district-report-card grades. Stakeholders' expectations are an integral and political part of what we do as educators. Nevertheless, Other-Centered Purpose must be maintained during these times of highly rational and quantitative accountability to sustain progress through Personal and Organizational Transformation.

Local-level test results are a third way to review, dissect, and analyze student performance. Through a careful disaggregation of student data by subject area, grade level, building, teacher, and student gender and race, educators may target specific areas of improvement, work together to provide instruction and support to students who are struggling in the targeted areas, and improve results (i.e., test scores) in these targeted areas. Important local knowledge is generated when teachers and teacher educators work together, systematically investigate, make accessible to critique by other professionals, and report back to the community the results of such study (Cochran-Smith & Lytle, 1993). Working together is a form of the Other-Centered Purpose that we espouse, and its capacity to sustain positive responses to the community is invaluable.

We find nothing in the previous accountability practices to preclude **Other-Centered Purpose** based on **Trust** and **Empowering Relationships.** We fully acknowledge the need for a public school system, which technically is a subdivision of the state legislature, to meet the political expectations of the community and the state and to perform efficaciously by producing the results desired by stakeholders. What we do challenge is the mistaken assumption that sustained improvement and results consistently will occur in organizations where Trust, Empowering Relationships, and Other-Centered Purpose are absent.

THE NEED FOR HUMILITY AND EXPANDING OTHER-CENTEREDNESS IN AN ORGANIZATION

To have an Other-Centered Purpose (as well as Trust), every person in an organization must focus on humility as a prerequisite to having faith and trust in another. We recall the work of Jourard (1971), who states that self-disclosure is the first step to acting with humility. It also is a step in trusting and confiding in another.

Humility is the core of Other-Centered Purpose. Humility is an emptying out of one's ego and self-interests to make room for other-centered interests including an intense focus on students. An analogy of a vessel into which one pours water is appropriate here. If one fills the vessel to a level of three-quarters full, there obviously remains space for another one quarter of fluid. But if the intent is to be able to pour in an amount of vegetable oil equal to one half of the volume of the vessel, then approximately one quarter of the vessel's water must be emptied out to make room in the top half for the vegetable oil. Likewise it is the same with humility and the emptying out of one's ego and self-interests. To make room for Other-Centered Purpose, organizational members first must shed some degree of ego, self-interests, and selfishness.

Selfishness and unselfishness are self-evidently opposites. The problem with selfishness in the workplace is that it leads to a lack of sharing and an unhealthy and, possibly, inordinate amount of pride in individual achievements at the expense of others' accomplishments. In a way, it is the opposite of what Sergiovanni (1994) espouses in his discussion of professional learning communities. However, unselfishness and humility are at the core of professional sharing in a learning community. Thus, an unselfish Other-Centered Purpose, if embraced by all staff members, could lead to a professional culture conducive of the learning communities Sergiovanni describes.

As previously stated, an unhealthy amount of pride is the result of selfishness. The problem with pride is that it can be counterproductive because of its two parts: self-justification and self-protection (B. Chouinard, personal communication, July 11, 2003).

Self-justification results when one resents another's work for a variety of reasons (e.g., a colleague receives an award, or a comment is made about another teacher's outstanding ability). When this resentment happens, one tries to justify to oneself why it is okay to resent and not to excuse or forgive the other person (Senge, 1990). Humility gives each member of the organization the freedom to say, "Sometimes I am not the only person with the best way of doing things."

One example of the need for humility versus self-justification is in the new "knowledge work" (Schlechty, 1997, p. 41) that teachers are asked to create for their students. According to this theory, such work that students do will result in a higher level of meaning and engagement if the students' needs and interests are taken into consideration with the design of each lesson. Through inquiry-based instruction, students' discoveries may help them to uncover content and meaning that have yet to be discovered even by the teacher. Humility is needed, then, by the teacher to accept what the students have learned and to acknowledge that the discovery may be new even to that teacher. Specifically, humility is needed in this role reversal where the student teaches the teacher.

Self-protection results when one responds to pressure to "play the game" the way everybody else does. For example, we may decide to not tell the truth because we would suffer loss of status or be ridiculed in some way. Therefore, one may avoid the deep issues and play the game out of self-protection. Humility gives each member the freedom to dispense with self-protection and to say, "I will trust in others regardless of the consequence, because there are plenty of others to speak on my behalf in my absence."

> **Focus Group Response**
>
> "It's amazing what can get done when nobody gets the credit."

Consider this actual case study of a nearby district's curriculum committee whose charge was to analyze the format of interim reports in a grading period. Discussions were going well, and all committee members were accepting of the need to modify what had been done in the past. New suggestions for other formats were openly shared in an environment of Other-Centered Purpose based on Trust and Empowering Relationships. The administrator in charge arrived to the meeting late, and when she discovered what was happening, she criticized the committee's work and redirected the outcome of the discussion. Committee members immediately went into a mode of self-protection. The real issue of their lack of relationships with this administrator never surfaced in the subsequent discussion about details to the new format. Of course, the real organizational damage occurred in the many conversations in the district staff lunchrooms on subsequent days and weeks. Other-Centered Purpose was damaged by a lack of Trust and lack of Empowering Relationships among the committee members and, vicariously, among the rest of the professional staff.

In the Managerial Domain, where routine, day-to-day issues are the norm and where the cycle of the Humane Dimension's components may not be readily detectable, any member of the organization may say, "I just want to play the game," and "I do not want to deal with the real issues." One may say that self-justification and self-protection are attributes of a lack of humility, and that these two attributes "grease the wheels of the mundane."

Of course, the problem with the lack of humility is that this lack can become a barrier to Personal Transformation (described in the next section). Stated differently, pride can prevent school improvement, reform, and, ultimately, transformation of the organization's members and culture.

Other-Centered Purpose based on Trust and Empowering Relationships are prerequisites to Personal Transformation. Without the thoughtful implementation of the cycle of the first three components of the Humane Dimension, lasting Transformation that is Personal and Organizational is nearly impossible.

OTHER-CENTERED PURPOSE AS A COMMUNITY BUILDER THROUGH SENSEMAKING

A final value, and probably most important contribution, of Other-Centered Purpose in schools is its capacity to support the growth and development of individuals and groups in the organization. Specifically, we examine its capacity to develop people and strengthen their commitment to pursue common goals and shared meanings.

In his book on the social construction of perspective, *Sensemaking in Organizations,* Weick (1995) elaborates implicitly on the details of other-centeredness. He argues that sensemaking, which is the human process of placing items into frameworks and comprehending things, "is never solitary because what a person does internally is contingent on others" (p. 40) and that "socialization is often the setting in which sensemaking is explored" (p. 40). Making sense through interactions with others is the core of Weick's thesis and of our claim that Other-Centered Purpose is an integral component in the cycle leading to Personal Transformation.

Conversation, then, is the primary vehicle for both sensemaking and developing Other-Centered Purpose. Weick (1995) states, "People who study sensemaking pay a lot of attention to talk, discourse, and conversation because that is how a great deal of social contact is mediated" (p. 41). Through discussions, common interests and goals are shared. Connections among individuals, described by Putnam (2000) as *social capital,* do increase. These commonalities and connections are the basis of community. And a professional learning community is the basis for the growth of the teaching profession as a whole (Sergiovanni, 1994).

Daily behavioral routines that affect the success of an organization reflect habits of the mind and heart that have grown out of socially constructed relationships. Weick (1995) observes that such patterns are a function of mutual experiences:

> When the same people show up day after day at the same time and place, their activities are likely to become more mutually defined, more mutually dependent, more mutually predictable, and more subject to common understanding encoded into common language. (p. 74)

This point is similar to one made by Sergiovanni (1994) regarding *Gemeinschaft* communities, where bonding of people results from mutual binding to common goals and shared values.

A final point about Weick's (1995) sensemaking in organizations is that its importance is based on how the sentient mind of humans in an organization learns—through relationships built by social construction. We believe this concept is the most cogent description of Other-Centered

Purpose that we have studied. Individuals' commitment to each other expands from this learning process through a focusing of attention on each other through conversation, by an uncovering of previously unnoticed features, and through a sharing of values. We end this section with Weick's important summary of this notion:

> Sensemaking is about the enlargement of small cues. It is a search for contexts within which small details fit together and make sense. It is a continuous alternation between particulars and explanations, with each cycle giving added form and substance to the other. (p. 133)

His previously described identification of a *cycle* in sensemaking is strongly related to our cycle of the four components of the Humane Dimension described in Chapter 1.

IMPLICATIONS FOR PRACTICE

Suggestions From Practitioners
on Other-Centered Purpose

Just as the Humane Dimension is a cycle of relationship-building components, so is the cycle of organizational transformation a process of culture-building steps. Practitioners from our focus groups have suggested the following model to promote Other-Centered Purpose.

Planting the Seeds (Today) . . . The Acorn

In January, a veteran Director of Staff Development in the Metropolitan City School District approaches her superintendent with a request to pilot a new teacher appraisal process. She explains that the process will emphasize voluntary participation, self-initiated teacher growth, and self-reflection on practice. The superintendent commits to working with the teachers' association to agree on the terms and conditions of the pilot. Subsequent to this agreement, the director invites teachers to participate in this pilot of alternative teacher appraisal next year. In the invitation, she emphasizes that the whole focus will not be on her, the appraiser, but rather on each teacher who agrees to participate; she states in her letter, "This pilot is all about **you**, your growth, and your professional interests!"

Searching for First Results (Short-Term) . . . The Seedling

About one third of Metropolitan City School District's teachers respond to the director's initial invitation. Her first action is to distribute *Cognitive Coaching* (Costa & Garmston, 1994), a book about teacher growth through a coaching model. She asks all volunteers to read the book over summer vacation. When the teachers return to a new school year in August, all teachers share the same knowledge about the importance of coaching in an alternative teacher appraisal process. The importance of each teacher's self-reflection is understood to be the focus.

Looking for Growth (Intermediate-Term) . . . The Sapling

The first pilot year of alternative teacher appraisal is perceived by all stakeholders to be successful. Teachers report that the appraiser's focus is entirely on them: their growth and their self-reflection. Also, they report that their own metacognition or self-monitoring is emphasized by their coach (i.e., appraiser). When the director of staff development reissues a new invitation to all teachers in May, about one half of Metropolitan City School District's teachers respond. Again, her first action is to distribute *Cognitive Coaching* (Costa & Garmston, 1994) and to ask all who are new to this appraisal process to read the book over the summer.

Transforming the Culture (Long-Term) . . . The Oak Tree

The second pilot year of alternative teacher appraisal is perceived to be even more successful than the prior year's pilot. Collegiality between teachers and administrators is experienced by all, and professional discussions are shared more freely in a variety of contexts. In May, the Metropolitan Educators' Association (MEA) requests that the new alternative teacher appraisal system be added permanently to the contract so that in the future, any teacher may ask to be appraised with a coaching model. More than one half of the teachers are expected to use this alternative in the subsequent school year. Through collaboration with the MEA, what was once a pilot now has become a systemic change.

APPLYING THE HUMANE DIMENSION

Specific staff development activities for developing Other-Centered Purpose are provided in the Professional Development Notepad exercises of Resource C.

REFLECTION

Q: Based on what you know about Other-Centered Purpose, think about your own school setting. Where are there moments or evidence of unselfish other-centeredness?

Q: Where would you like to see more effort toward achieving Other-Centered Purpose?

Q: What are some ideas that you have to *start* this important work?

Q: What strategies might teachers try to *cultivate and sustain* Other-Centered Purpose?

Q: What strategies might building principals and district administrators try to *cultivate and sustain* Other-Centered Purpose?

Q: In what ways can *you* help now to *initiate and cultivate* Other-Centered Purpose in *your* building culture? In your district culture?

5

Humane Dimension Component 4

Personal and Organizational Transformation

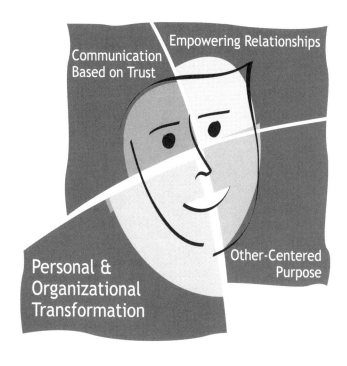

Every act leaves the world with a deeper or a fainter impress of God.

—A. N. Whitehead, *Religion in the Making* (1926)

Personal Transformation and Organizational Transformation make up the fourth step in the Humane Dimension cycle. What do these phenomena look like? Exact descriptions may be elusive, but step into a public school classroom at any level from preschool through the twelfth grade, and when students are genuinely engrossed in their work, there is a sort of majestic hum that is music to every teacher's ear. Asked to describe common, everyday evidence that their students are engaged in meaningful classroom work, teachers at one high school identified not-too-surprising traits such as the following:

- Students are smiling as they work with each other.
- Students challenge each other.
- They are asking questions that lead to more questions.
- Students use information presented to improve and enhance their work.
- They push the teacher to improve.
- Students share their work with others because they are proud of it.

Evident in this picture is a coming together of individuals—their ideas, their personalities, their spirits. Teachers know when this happens; much of their work is aimed at making this happen. Yet time and time again, what teachers want for their students, this sense of relating to others for a higher good, escapes the adults who work in schools. Their desire to change the classroom culture and to be changed themselves is elusive. At the very edge of this desire is the potential for Personal Transformation of each student, teacher, and administrator in the school. And just beyond this edge of the Personal Transformation of each individual is the potential for Organizational Transformation of the school.

As we will discuss in detail later in this book, schools are organizations that are typically managed according to corporate sensibilities. Over the past century, as a result of population growth, increased immigration, attendance mandates, federal regulations for handicapped students, and professional credentialing, the one-room schoolhouse, by sheer necessity, turned to the corporate world as a model for efficiency and development.

This observation is not meant to be derisive of all that is connected to the business world. As schools and school districts grew over the past 50 years, decisions had to be made about hiring practices, budgets, and curriculum. Building maintenance alone required management as did busing of students. In order for teachers to have the time to teach students, someone had to be in charge. That schools must be organized is not the problem. Nor is it a problem that we have adopted many organizational practices such as overspecialization, isolation, and role rigidity. The problem is that too many people in the organization called a school system no longer know how to (or even care to) relate to each other as human beings.

The field of organization development began in the early years of U.S. corporate growth. Organization development is an interdisciplinary approach that incorporates the learning of business, sociology, and psychology and applies this knowledge to organization life. In the late 1980s, organization development branched out with a new approach called Organizational Transformation (Schaef & Fassel, 1988). While organization development examined how organizations could be more productive, Organizational Transformation examined a broader question tangled in the complexities of human relatedness. Organizational Transformation asked, "How can the world be different as a result of the responsibility we take in it and our participation with it?" (p. 31). Oden (1999) saw Organizational Transformation as a "complete and radical change in strategy, culture, structure, and processes" that will not occur through a mere series of "incremental changes" (p. ix).

Embedded in the literature of paradigm shifts, Organizational Transformation sees the shift in organizational life dependent on debunking the myth of objectivity and unveiling the illusions of the logical positivism and empiricism in the workplace. These illusions, while sustaining organizations as smooth-running machines, lead to the estrangement of the people who work within them.

Organizational Transformation focuses on bringing people within organizations back together in ways that transcend everyday (or workday) language. What do we call the sense of connectedness when a group of people accomplishes something bigger than itself? Are there terms in our organizations for that fleeting sense of awe we experience when we are lifted beyond our common insecurities by another person's simple act of compassion? The language of faith certainly could be used to describe these experiences. But public schools are secular organizations where religious beliefs usually are not espoused. In order for the organization of schools to move beyond reforming to transforming, we will have to acknowledge the human spirit that toils in our buildings. Whether we ascribe that spirit to a higher power or we base it on individual expressions of humanity, school practitioners have to see the need to move from what we call the Managerial Domain to the Humane Dimension.

We believe that the fourth and primary element of the Humane Dimension is Personal and Organizational Transformation. Ferguson (1980) had this in mind in her description of an "imminent transformation" under way in our society. She described this transformation as "a matrix of linked beliefs—that we are invisibly joined to one another, that there are dimensions transcending time and space, that individual lives are meaningful, that grace and illumination are real, that it is possible to evolve to ever higher levels of understanding" (p. 61).

SYSTEMIC DEVELOPMENT VERSUS ORGANIZATIONAL TRANSFORMATION

Much of the literature of recent school reform focuses on the development of the system. The notion of systemic development suggests the idea of discrete components of a system beginning to work together as a refined whole. So we analyze those components for their strengths and their weaknesses to rebuild the organization into a more synergized whole. Translated into educational language, we look at various levels within the organization, most commonly administration, classroom teachers, and classified staff. These levels are further dissected according to decision-making power so that, for instance, the central office administrators are distinguished from building-level administrators, and program directors are distinguished from program supervisors. Systemic development activities usually include an assessment phase followed by some form of strategic planning.

Assessment of a System

Assessing a school system rarely gets to the heart of the potential for change in a school district—that is, the Personal Transformation of the individuals who make up the organization—because individual voices are often ignored. Instead, a long-term assessment of a school district asks questions aimed at components:

- How do administrators support classroom teachers' attempts to improve student learning?
- In what ways does the board of education support the central office?
- How do classroom teachers typically communicate with parents?
- What kinds of professional development opportunities are available for certified staff?

We do understand the motivation behind assessing a system. Typically, boards of education and management are sure that they must lead and set the organization's goals and that the rest of the constituents should follow. As well, the sheer number of individuals in even a moderately sized school district (e.g., approximately 600 employees and 4,000 students in the Kent City School District) creates a practical dilemma of gathering data, analyzing information, and drawing conclusions about what path should be taken to improve schools. For example, should we ask each individual about the current status and future directions of the district? (Of course, we do ask, but the synthesis of information into simple solutions becomes the problem.) So, evaluating system components in the context of a set of standards is a more available and accessible path to take.

Argyris (1999a) recommends that assessing and changing a system could be accomplished by examining employees' perspectives and, ultimately, "altering their individual theories of action that lead them [i.e., practitioners] to produce the automatic responses" (p. 93). Routines of current behavior are compared to a rubric of desired behaviors in a discrepancy analysis. Through this analysis, individuals experience *important learning.* Argyris writes, "By *important learning* I mean learning that goes beyond understanding and explanation to producing desired changes and, therefore, learning new values and skills as well as creating new kinds of social systems" (p. 104).

We accept this focus on behaviors and routines, and we acknowledge an organization's desire to modify such, where necessary. As stated in Chapter 1, however, the Humane Dimension is only one piece of a complex puzzle of organizational change and transformation. It especially examines the hidden part of individuals' performance, that which is motivated by relationships and trust and the part that needs attention to accomplish change that is lasting.

Strategic Planning of a System

The answers to these questions are analyzed and turned into goals in the form of some sort of strategic plan. By the time members of each distinct group within the organization shift through the collected data, and competing interests of individuals and groups are integrated into a final report, what remains is an amorphous, innocuous collection of recommendations. The recommendations for nearly any single school district in this country could just as easily be adopted by any number of other school districts because, in effect, what is left is the lowest common denominator of reform. The fewer the toes that are stepped on, the more palatable the plan. We aim for what we can live with and then wonder why little has changed in our schools.

Transformation

The traditional school reform assessment and subsequent planning remain confined to the Managerial Domain because they ignore what makes individual lives meaningful (i.e., Personal Transformation).

How would a school's faculty react to a study that posed questions like these?

- How has your commitment to working with students evolved over the past five years?
- What keeps you coming back to work with our students?

- Describe the adults in this building/district who foster your commitment to our students.
- Describe the adults in this building/district who weaken your commitment to our students.

Personal and Organizational Transformation, as opposed to systemic development, is at the core of the change that we suggest. Instead of examining the discrete functions of an organization's separate components, its relational aspects are unveiled. Ethical and moral questions are not considered "fuzzy religious concepts but key elements in our relationships with staff, suppliers, and stakeholders" (Wheatley, 1992, p. 12). Leadership is not viewed as a position within the organization but is examined for its relational aspects like "followship, empowerment, and leader accessibility" (p. 14).

PASSION FOR IDEAS VERSUS COMPASSION FOR PEOPLE

Reforming schools within the Managerial Domain, in contrast to transforming schools within the Humane Dimension, traditionally follows a sequence of district assessment, strategic planning, and, finally, reform activities. These reform activities are paraded out under a banner or in some sort of kickoff event. Some districts initiate their reform activities internally with convocation day speakers, videotapes, and posters. Other districts begin their "era of reform" with public relations events like newscasts, city club addresses, and newspaper coverage. Whether the kickoff is internal, external, or both, the approach requires a theme that can rally the majority of the stakeholders and inspire them with the fervor of reform. Over the past decade, reform themes that have captivated districts around the country include "All Children Can Learn," "No Child Left Behind," and "Working on the Work."

There is nothing essentially wrong with these themes. What parents don't want to hear that their children's academic success is at the core of their school's work? What teachers or administrators don't want their efforts at helping students learn affirmed? The cause is noble; it is both moral and right. But, in time, it pales. The banner begins to droop within the first two or three years of reform. Teachers feel left out. Administrators feel abandoned. Parents become voiceless. Who is responsible for this predictable pattern? Is it the board of education? Is it the central office administrators? Is it the state department of education? Or might it be the federal government?

It is our contention that blame cannot be placed on any of these groups. Their passions, our passions, for students and their learning were noble, moral, and right. But when we artificially squeezed fervor for an idea onto a banner, we took the easy way out of the complexities of human emotions. We replaced compassion for people with passion for an idea.

People who work in schools know the daily frustrations of limited time to do quality work. Mandated programs, necessary remediation, jammed curriculum, and so on crowd out the day. Teachers and administrators cling to their district's banner of reform as a mantra underscoring real, meaningful change. Educators who adopt the reform theme do so with their own interpretation of what that change will mean. For the primary teacher, reform could mean more time to plan interdisciplinary units with special area teachers. The middle school principal may envision developing better links to the high school curriculum. And the high school guidance counselor may view reform as the inroad to collaboration with community mental health agencies. Within a year or two, the passion for the idea, motto, or banner diminishes as individual visions of change are thwarted by inevitable barriers like lack of time, reduced spending, increased graduation requirements, and, most important, lack of trust—in the system and in each other.

A passion for _____ (insert reform motto here) is a commitment to an idea that could never really be shared. People have unfathomable motives. They dream individual dreams. It is the ignoring of these motives and dreams that time and time again undermines even the best reform goals. Adrienne Rich (1976) once observed that those who have the authority to lead can "take a short-cut through the complexities of human personality" (p. 49).

In contrast to this passion for ideas is a compassion for people, a willingness to wade through the complexities of human personality. In our culture, leaders who embrace a passion for _____ (again, fill in the blank with any reform motto) must be strong and tenacious. They must be willing to sacrifice private time and personal commitments to the cause. They are expected to make the hard decisions. Meek individuals cannot take on the tasks of school reform and succeed. But could it be that this very description of a strong leader is contrary to the achievement of individuals' Personal Transformation that we espouse here? Perhaps our distaste for the word "meekness" has propelled us to hire and to cling to strong, tenacious, sacrificing leaders. What if we were, instead, to honor meekness as strength under control? What if we no longer associated meekness with fear or powerlessness but, instead, with faith?

FEAR VERSUS FAITH

In the Humane Dimension of school reform, faith would be a topic deliberately and openly discussed. Faith's counterpart in the Managerial Domain is fear—fear of appearing weak, of not doing a good enough job. In our culture, we mask fear with a myriad of personality traits. Some people swagger in smug displays of self-confidence. Some dismiss other people's ideas and concerns with cold, quiet judgment. Fear finds its way into the classroom where teachers second-guess their teaching skills until, eventually, they tune out any more messages of research findings aimed at reforming education. In the principal's office, fear masquerades as one-way communication and "telling, not deliberating." At the central office, fear mutes the voices of teachers and parents. Covey (1989) describes the "scarcity mentality" of people who fear that their supplies of power, recognition, and credit will be depleted by another person's success. Staff developers are fond of a story that illustrates this point. One afternoon, a southern gentleman was walking along a riverbank when he spotted a young boy catching crawfish. He watched as the boy placed each catch in an open bucket. "Son," the gentleman called out, "you better get you a lid for that bucket or all those crawfish are gonna crawl out." The boy replied, "Mister, you don't know much about crawfish. As soon as one gets near the top of the bucket, the other ones will pull it down."

Out of fear, we educators often can pull each other down. We hide our talents behind closed doors. We hoard information. In organizations, information is considered power. The more an individual knows, the more powerful he deems himself to be. This practice is unlike that found in a professional learning community (Sergiovanni, 1994). During major reform, information should be free-flowing among all constituents, the administrators, the board of education, teachers, parents, and other community members. Typically, though, the data collected during a district self-study end up being filtered away, and this depiction depends on who does what with the information. Again, fear raises its ugly head in the Managerial Domain.

TRADITIONAL SILO STRUCTURES VERSUS PROFESSIONAL LEARNING COMMUNITIES

Another way is possible. Covey (1989) contrasts the scarcity mentality with the abundance mentality, "the paradigm that there is plenty out there and enough to spare for everybody. It results in sharing of prestige, of recognition, of profits, of decision making. It opens possibilities, options, alternatives, and creativity" (p. 220). Undergirding this paradigm is a faith in other people and in their intentions. In the Humane Dimension, individual and group fear is diminished by individual and group faith, by Personal and Organizational Transformation. Civility, caring, and connectedness define our relationships with one another. We treat other people with respect. We reach outside of our independent worlds (i.e., silos) and connect our ideas in a way that everyone can grow (i.e., professional learning communities). A passion for an idea becomes balanced by a compassion for people.

PERSONAL AND ORGANIZATIONAL TRANSFORMATION

Invisibly Joined to One Another

In a short story titled "Edification/Demolition," Wangerin (1984) describes two encounters at two different self-service gas stations. At one, the attendant greeted him at the pump, smiling and patient as he waited for payment. The attendant acknowledged Wangerin's young son in the back-seat of the car with a grin and left the scene with a handshake and a smile. At the second gas station, the attendant waited miserably inside at her desk. She did not make eye contact with Wangerin and responded to his offer of money with a brusque "Whaddaya want me to do with that?" Sullenness and anger oozed from her words and from her silence. Wangerin noted that he left the first encounter with joy and the second with sorrow. He was edified at the first gas station and demolished at the second.

This gas station narrative briefly illustrates how people are invisibly joined to one another. By our actions, words, moods, silences, and so on, we have the capacity to edify or to demolish each other. In schools we do this in face-to-face encounters, within groups, and behind each other's backs. In any one of these social situations, each individual has the choice to aim for a higher good through Personal Transformation or to settle for self-satisfaction. Edification has nothing to do with the "nice talk" that is all too common among adults in and out of schools. That kind of pander-ing and skirting around the serious issues is at best, superficial and at worst, duplicitous. Edification between two educators occurs when honest communication about legitimate pedagogical concerns takes place. Two teachers discussing a genuine struggle with measuring student learning can be the building blocks of authentic assessment. A group of district administrators and various departments making deep cuts in the district's budget could be involved in an edifying experience if turfism and self-interests were put aside for the greater good of the system. And each time a person withholds a disparaging comment about an absent colleague because it just might not be true, a greater good is served, and trust grows between these two people and within the organization. In fact, the greatest good is that trust grows, Personal Transformation occurs, and Organizational Transformation becomes possible.

Collins (2001) addresses the piece-by-piece nature of organizational change through transformation. He states,

No matter how dramatic the end result, the good-to-great transfor-mations never happened in one fell swoop. There was no single defining action, no grand program, no one killer innovation, no solitary lucky break, no miracle moment. Rather, the process resembled relentlessly pushing a giant heavy flywheel in one direction, turn upon turn, building momentum until a point of breakthrough, and beyond. (p. 14)

Dimensions That Transcend Time and Space

The Managerial Domain of traditional school reform efforts is a flat (and often spiritless) place, unless it is enhanced by the cycle of relationship building in the Humane Dimension. Its systemic elements may be necessary but are not sufficient for personal and school transformation to take place. The two dimensions of time and space aptly describe the ordinary school setting. It can be said that each educator's worth is measured by time and space. The length of a career span often indicates value. So people rise through the ranks according to their tenacity to "stay the course." It could even be said that individual worth is measured by the length of one's workday. Putting in long hours is for some reason equated with talent and sacrifice.

> ### Focus Group Response
>
> "People are happy with what they are doing; they want to come to school. There is a sense of completion of a task, of a job well done."

The other dimension, space, may also be used to measure the worth of an individual in schools. Because they do not always have a classroom of their own, new teachers are often forced to travel from room to room. The sight of them pushing their carts filled with books, journals, assignments, and other materials can elicit sympathy from veteran staff. In schools with multiple principals, the bigger and better office typically belongs to the top administrator. And at the central office, size and site of office space can determine status.

When we adhere only to time and space as standards of worth, we exist in the Managerial Domain, a flat ordinariness. When we attempt to reform our schools within the confines of these two dimensions, we perpetuate the illusion of what is worthy. We assess the condition of our school district and replace a program or two; perhaps we restructure or even create a few positions.

> ### Focus Group Response
>
> "We quit treating each other as if we are positions because we have a common goal."

But we are assured of ordinariness when we evaluate these programs and these positions by the length of time they last and by the space they fill. Hall's (1995) work on understanding the concept of an innovation reveals the following:

- Conditions, in addition to time and space, must be altered and supported as well (e.g., role changes, rule removals, expanded vision).
- Developmental shifts in individual perspectives must be documented.
- Collegial research must be embedded in innovations.

It is our belief that another dimension, the Humane Dimension, should be included in our attempts to transform individuals and education. We operate in the Humane Dimension when we look beyond time and space to find the worth in the people around us. When we become capable of taking on multiple perspectives of an event or of a person, we move beyond the flatness of our presuppositions and learn to relate. It is in relationship that we learn to strive for a higher good. Teachers who connect in genuine ways with their students know this. Faculty members who act out of concern for each other know this, too. When these educators begin to see that this higher good is more attainable in relationship, school transformation can take place.

> **Focus Group Response**
>
> "People are aware of their passions and share their passions with others. Teachers' dialogue is about learning, about educational practices, and not about other groups of people. There is forgiveness over the mistakes we all make."

Teachers experience personal transformation through a variety of professional development adjustments such as common planning times, community collaborations, grade-level meetings, and partner observations. After a series of face-to-face encounters with other teachers who experience similar adjustments, the culture of a few individuals is transformed.

IMPLICATIONS FOR PRACTICE

Suggestions From Practitioners on Personal and Organizational Transformation

Just as the Humane Dimension is a cycle of relationship-building components, so is the cycle of organizational transformation a process of culture-building steps. Practitioners from our focus groups have suggested the following model to promote Personal and Organizational Transformation.

Planting the Seeds (Today) . . . The Acorn

After a yearlong examination of data, which included standardized test scores, textbook assessments, and teacher records, the faculty at one elementary building set the following goal: In three years, at least 75% of all sixth-grade students will pass the Sixth-Grade Math Proficiency Test.

Over the summer, three teachers from the second, fourth, and sixth grades agree to attend a series of classes and workshops on standards-based math instruction and assessment. Their responsibility for the fall is to share what they have learned with the rest of the faculty in lunchtime presentations and afterschool mini-workshops. The principal designs teachers' schedules to ensure common lunch times and common planning times for all grade-level teachers. One of the three "lead math teachers" is able to meet at least twice each week with grade-level groups. The principal covers classes when needed.

Searching for First Results (Short-Term) . . . The Seedling

By the second semester, the teachers agree that the series of presentations and mini-workshops facilitated by the lead math teachers are successful. They want to make changes in their math instruction and suggest that classroom observations would help. In particular, teachers want to observe the lead math teachers teaching math either in their own classrooms or in other teachers' classrooms. More coverage is needed so the faculty agrees to "buy" substitute teaching time by combining two spring field trips and reducing two schoolwide assemblies to one. The principal agrees to cover three classes a week, and other teachers step in to cover during their planning periods.

Looking for Growth (Intermediate-Term) . . . The Sapling

By the beginning of the second year, test results confirm that students are achieving more in math. The three lead math teachers receive advanced training and expand professional development opportunities to the faculty. Along with study groups, workshops, and classroom observations, grade-level teams work with one of the lead math teachers to plan lessons and units. Each month, each grade-level team and leader are released from their classrooms to plan. Data from tests and teacher observations are used in these planning sessions. To provide classroom coverage for these half-day planning sessions, special area instruction (physical education, art, and music) coincide with grade-level service projects. Community volunteers and parents who work with groups of students for two hours each month on service-learning topics and activities facilitate these projects.

Transforming the Culture (Long-Term) . . . The Oak Tree

At the end of the second year, the math goal is met. As the faculty prepares to work on the new language arts curriculum, the teachers recommend a duplication of the previous process. Three other teachers who have long been recognized as the building's "reading and writing gurus" volunteer to attend summer workshops and courses on reading instruction and writing instruction. The cycle continues.

APPLYING THE HUMANE DIMENSION

Specific staff development activities for developing Personal Transformation are provided in the Professional Development Notepad exercises of Resource D.

REFLECTION

Q: Based on what you know about Personal Transformation, think about your own school setting. Where are there moments or evidence of transformation?

Q: Where would you like to see more effort toward achieving Personal Transformation?

Q: What are some ideas that you have to *start* this important work?

Q: What strategies might teachers try to *cultivate and sustain* Personal Transformation?

Q: What strategies might building principals and district administrators try to *cultivate and sustain* Personal Transformation?

Q: In what ways can *you* help now to *initiate and cultivate* Personal Transformation in *your* building culture? In your district culture?

6

Elements of a Transformed Leadership Culture

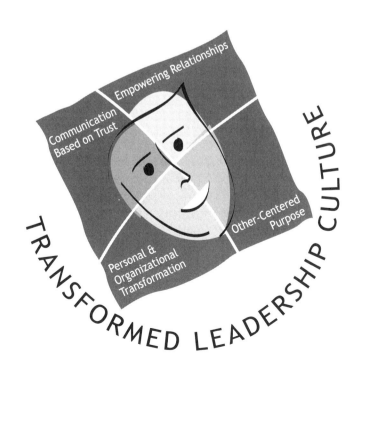

In Chapter 1's "Landscape of the School," members of Roosevelt's School Improving Team (SIT) described a time when Personal Transformation flourished in the 1990s. Subsequent to that time, the Roosevelt staff had been engaged in a process of appreciative inquiry (Cooperrider & Whitney, 1999). During the 2003–2004 school year, results of the inquiry were documented and assessed. These notes included an acknowledgment and description of specific elements in Roosevelt's transformed organizational culture.

For purposes of simplicity and clarity, we have divided our presentation of a transformed culture into two parts: leadership transformation and teacher transformation (i.e., Chapters 6 and 7, respectively).

What we have observed at Roosevelt is a group of elements in the transformed organization that seem to flourish in an environment of constant recycling of the Humane Dimension's components. Our observation is that the recurring components of the Dimension support the success of these leadership and teacher culture elements.

We begin this section on a transformed leadership culture with the premise that the focus of the transformed leader is the growth and support of others, so that they may have a positive influence on the students and staff in their school. In turn, through this ethic of growth and support, the school district and the surrounding community at large benefit from the impact of these individuals' efforts. Thus, a response to the following question by Greenleaf (1998) emerges from the collective actions and words that thrive in this climate of improvement and support that is promoted by the transformed leader:

> The generation of a shared vision may be one of those wonderful things that just happens when genuine respect for persons, for all persons, is consistently manifested. Within the climate of that pervasive attitude, and in the normal course of decision making, the first response of both the key leader and all subordinate leaders may be the simple question, "What are we trying to do?" (p. 79)

The primary emphasis of a transformed leader is to build a team of leaders who are going in the same direction based on the similar belief that a leader's main focus is to serve and support the growth of others. An appropriate vision will emerge from this emphasis. The simplicity of this premise, however, escapes many leaders. One only needs to look around at the many leadership practices, styles, and purposes found in organizations where support and growth are not emphasized.

We proceed now with our observations of a transformed administrative culture at Roosevelt High School. Specifically, we see the following four elements:

- Team first/vision later
- Constructivist practices for administrators

- Participatory leadership structures
- Win/win consensus building, negotiating, and decision making

ELEMENT 1: TEAM FIRST/VISION LATER

The single most important element of a transformed leadership culture is *teamwork.* Sergiovanni (1994) refers to this element as *building community.* When leaders in a culture consider themselves members of a team, their limits of commitment to the organization, dedication to the professional community, and love of children are maximized. Note that the leaders of the culture must consider themselves members of the team. It does no good for one or two leaders to try to bestow or empower a sense of team membership among all the others. Stated differently, leaders must be able to empower themselves with the freedom to commit, dedicate, and love. This empowerment must emerge individually and authentically from the heart and soul of each team member. External empowerment is an oxymoron (see our discussion on empowerment in Chapter 3).

Recently, on a local public television broadcast for Memorial Day, many stories were told by soldiers who were veterans in the ground battles of World War II. Although the initial motivation for their service in the infantry division may have been a sense of patriotic duty to their flag and country, the ultimate motivation for leaving the safety of their foxholes and advancing forward as a group into dangerous combat was their commitment to each other. At those moments of maximum threat to their lives and safety, they relied on the ethic of caring for and protecting each other as their main reasons for jeopardizing their own lives.

The empowerment and freedom previously described are functions of two specific sources: truthfulness to each other and similarity in beliefs about what is important to each person individually and to the team as a whole. The remainder of this section on team first/vision later focuses on these two sources.

Truthfulness to Each Other: The First Source of Team

Senge (1990) discusses a commitment to truth in an organization, the first source of empowerment in a team. This commitment requires truthfulness in all transactions and interactions. It does not take long for one leader to determine that another leader is untruthful. This lack of truth is an atomic devastation to the team. Recurring transgressions of truthfulness lower the credibility of a leader almost to a point of no recovery. In short, truthfulness to each other is necessary for a team to exist. Lack of truthfulness, including omissions of truth from the team, can result in a total and irrevocable disintegration of teamwork.

Barwick (1990) lists trust and respect as prerequisites to the interdependence of team members. Truthfulness is at the core of trust and respect. Other leadership traits such as ability, creativity, personality, and vision cannot replace truthfulness as the foundation for trust and respect.

> ### Focus Group Response
>
> "Individual agendas are set aside in the interest of the whole group."

Collins (2001) provides an important action in developing respect among peers and subordinates. He states that a great leader "looks out the window, not the mirror, to apportion credit for the success of the company to other people" (p. 36).

Similarity in Beliefs About What Is Important: The Second Source of Team

The second source of team empowerment and freedom to commit, dedicate, and love in an organization is similarity among leaders in beliefs and in what is important. This similarity is a result of refined personnel practices that support the recruitment, selection, retention, and development of people who have similarities in their beliefs about what is important in the organization and what their ultimate purpose is in the organization. Like a lack of truthfulness, a lack of similarity in beliefs can result in a total and irrevocable disintegration of teamwork.

We pause here to address a hypothetical challenge to the concept of similarity in beliefs by our critics in the form of a question: What better similar purpose could exist than the achievement of students, and could this similarity alone be sufficient to override all other dissimilarities? Although we understand intuitively what this question is asking about students, nevertheless we must respond to this question in the negative. In the adult cultures of administrators and teachers, personal agendas and power struggles may have significantly more capacity to motivate professional behavior than the singular motive of assisting students with their achievement. Ignoring this phenomenon could be a very naive and overly simplistic assumption for anyone to make. The altruistic argument that students alone should be the only motivation for action by an educator ignores how many adults function in an organization. Simply consider the notion that not every educator went into teaching to influence students' lives.

The Structured Interview

Refined personnel practices include the use of a valid and reliable structured interview that can help determine the extent to which an individual leader may hold beliefs and goals that are congruent with those of the organization and team. Several sources of such structured interviews currently exist for school organizations. We point the reader to the structured interviews of Cardinal and Associates (1985), the Gallup Organization's (i.e., formerly Selection Research Instruments [SRI]) Teacher Perceiver Instrument (TPI), Ventures for Excellence, and Talent Plus Quality Selection Process. All of these sources may be found by a search engine of the World Wide Web. Although all of these systems offer benefits for school organizations, we particularly focus here on the leader's structured interview of Cardinal.

The structured interview process assumes that certain traits are being sought by the leadership team. These traits are selected to match some ideal profile of a candidate of the leading or teaching position that is vacant. Questions are constructed to define and identify a core set of beliefs and behaviors in the candidate being interviewed (Brobeck, 1998). The ideal candidate's profile derives from field studies where responses by the "best" practitioners, as identified by peers, form the bases of the scoring rubric.

Numerous questions on each trait are asked sporadically throughout the interview. Subsequent to the interview's completion, the interviewer codes and scores the interviewee's taped responses to check for a match between what was actually said and the preferred or predicted response that was generally produced by the best practitioners in the field.

Certain assumptions go along with the use of a structured interview (Brobeck, 1998). One assumption is that the candidate is answering each question *honestly*. The interviewer generally is seeking consistency of responses related to each specific trait; this consistency is one bit of evidence that a candidate speaks with honesty. Another assumption is that candidates say automatically what they are thinking during the interview. That is, if a candidate neglects to say something, it is either that the omission is not within the candidate's experience or that the candidate simply forgot to say it. In either case, the interviewer is unable to predict the candidate's performance related to a specific trait.

Brobeck (1998) identifies several advantages of structured interviews as a selection tool. For example, structured interviews are a systematic method of selection. They can be valid, reliable, and consistent. They provide an objective and relatively scientific means of selecting personnel who consistently share the same altruistic traits. Finally, they are a cost-effective method of identifying core beliefs and behaviors of candidates.

Cardinal's (1985) Core Beliefs and Behaviors

Cardinal (1985) identifies the core beliefs and behaviors of various positions in school districts, such as superintendents, directors (e.g., curriculum), building administrators, department heads, teachers, coaches, counselors, and many support staff positions. For the purpose of brevity, our discussion is limited here to the core beliefs and behaviors of his interview for the administrator as leader.

We return momentarily to the premise that underpins the focus of a transformed leader: the growth and support of others, so that they may have a positive influence on the students and staff in their school. In turn, through this ethic of growth and support, the school district and the surrounding community at large benefit from the impact of these individuals' efforts. For all members of the leadership team to be heading in this same direction, which we are recommending, their efforts must be based on the similar belief that *a leader's main focus is to serve and support the growth of others.*

> ### Focus Group Response
>
> "There has to be a 'compassionate chain of command.' The flow of information is free and open. Ownership and responsibility are shared in good times and in bad. When mistakes happen, everyone shares in the work to correct it without judgment."

The previous premise is the essence of Cardinal's (1985) core beliefs and behaviors. In his set of twelve traits or core beliefs and behaviors, Cardinal consistently focuses on the growth of the individual. Thus, he refers to the following traits as competencies of outstanding administrators:

- *Purpose.* The administrator's purpose is to establish and maintain a positive environment that is most conducive to teaching and learning.
- *Delivery Focus.* The administrator directs significant energy in selecting and developing the group that directly delivers services to young people, namely, the teachers.
- *Growth Activator.* The administrator is the catalyst in a growth environment and sees that the major purpose of delegation is for the growth of the individual.
- *Performance Expectation.* The administrator operates from goals that have specific, measurable criteria, but tends to have an excellent understanding of the balance needed between the performer and performance.
- *Positive Work Ethic.* The administrator has a high work orientation, but maintains an excellent balance between home and work responsibilities.
- *Sensitivity.* The administrator is highly sensitive to the thoughts and feelings of others and shows consideration for others by seeking causes before moving to recommend or suggest solutions.
- *Communicator.* The administrator is an open and honest communicator and is highly skilled as a listener and speaker.
- *Organization/Preparation.* The administrator is highly organized and prepared and uses organization to benefit others.
- *Stability/Objectivity.* The administrator generates a feeling of confidence among those supervised and expresses appreciation for input to contributors after a decision has been made.

- *Positive Association.* The administrator is very aware of the value of positive relationships with all audiences and uses power and authority to establish an ongoing positive teaching and learning climate.
- *Concept of Total.* The administrator clearly understands how the parts make up the whole, and how the activity of one part can affect the whole; such thinking is global in nature. Therefore, the total overall climate of the district is of prime importance.
- *Self-Directed.* A mission of impacting society in positive ways is the primary life ambition of this administrator, whose life direction is *to serve others.*

With regard to implementing Cardinal's (1985) competencies of outstanding administrators, one final point must be addressed here: the capacity to make adjustments in the leadership team. In this context, we refer to the leadership team at large, to include board office administrators, building administrators, curriculum leaders, and all other teacher leaders.

After the initial structured interview has occurred, areas of growth should be identified and targeted in a growth plan or profile. When follow-up growth plans, interviews, and personal profiles have failed to result in sufficient growth and change, a hard decision unfortunately must be made. Members of a team perform at their best when no exceptions are made to this scenario. When any member of the leadership team is exempted from adhering to the beliefs, standards, and behaviors set by the team, action is needed. Allowing a team to remain as is when many members of the team are seeking action and change is a cancer that eventually eats away at the integrity (i.e., truthfulness) of the team.

The reverse situation of the cancer previously described is an effective team that is ready to address a vision process. Although we do not elaborate here on a specific vision process, we emphasize that a team that is committed to integrity and similar beliefs will not have difficulty with any vision process described in the literature. Such a team has been evident at Roosevelt High School for more than the past three decades, in spite of a natural cycle of turnover in teachers and administrators.

In summary, Collins (2001) contrasts the following difference between two different levels of leaders. Whereas a Level 4 leader first looks at *what* (i.e., set a vision) then *who* (i.e., crew of "helpers"), the Level 5 leader first looks at *who* (i.e., the right people) then *what* (i.e., the best path). This belief is consistent with Cardinal's (1985).

ELEMENT 2: CONSTRUCTIVIST PRACTICES FOR ADMINISTRATORS

Background

The struggle for personal and professional recognition in an organization is an important challenge to be addressed by a leader. On any given day in the organization, some desire and struggle for recognition will occur. This notion does not mean that every person in an organization is seeking an award or spotlight of some kind (i.e., extrinsic reward). Rather, it means that adults are seeking recognition of their own points of view, their own values (i.e., intrinsic reward). If the sum total of any adult's perspective is the accumulation of experiences, then adults working in the organization are simply seeking acknowledgment that their own lives, their life experiences, have validity and value to others.

Like the Golden Rule, reciprocal acknowledgment between adults forms the basis for healthy relationships. Deeper understandings of each other's practices, perspectives, and virtues become the foundation for assembling organizational aims that are enduring and are embraced by all employees. The constructivist leader is one whose first consideration is of others' perspectives and needs in determining where and how to place the building blocks of new knowledge on each person's foundation of learning experiences. The constructivist leader's focus must be to create an environment where other-centered recognition (i.e., versus self-centered recognition) is the core of the organization's daily modus operandi.

> **Focus Group Response**
>
> "Disagreement is okay and is worked through. Sarcasm is nonexistent. There is a sense of playfulness."

The leader's challenge, then, is to support others' professional development by providing them the opportunity to construct new knowledge on the building blocks of their life experiences. This support is what good teachers do with their students, what good department chairpersons do with their faculty, what good principals do with their staffs, and what good district leaders do with staff members under their jurisdiction. In short, this is what a constructivist does daily. Sizer (1992) states, "The governing metaphor of the school should be student as worker, rather than the more familiar metaphor of teacher as deliverer of instructional services" (p. 208). This comment reflects a constructivist's belief.

To better understand a follower's reactions to decisions, constructivist leaders must develop a self-awareness and understanding of their own perspectives, professional practices, and *virtues*. By developing such an understanding, the leader expands the capacity to better understand others' perspectives and practices, and to better recognize the virtues of those who are led.

Virtues of a Constructivist Leader

Our use of the term *virtue* here is not intended to be moralistic. Although multiple definitions of this term exist, we submit one dictionary definition that says *virtue* is the "power or property of producing a particular effect" (Barnhart, 1951). The effect which we seek is the cycle of human interactions that we describe as the Humane Dimension (viz., Communication Based on Trust, Empowering Relationships, Other-Centered-Purpose, and Personal and Organizational Transformation).

Thus, we espouse that organizational leaders—and we refer to leaders in the broadest sense of the term at all organizational levels—must possess certain virtues. The virtues that we have observed in constructivist leaders at Roosevelt High School are supportive of the components of the Humane Dimension. In the section that follows, each virtue is discussed in the context of a specific component.

Virtue 1: Servant Leadership (Supports Communication Based on Trust)

The virtue of Servant Leadership is supportive of the Humane Dimension's first component, namely, Communication Based on Trust. Evidence of this virtue may be found in the following behaviors of the constructivist leader, all of which are identified in Autry's (2002) work on servant-leadership:

- Does not try to control people
- Becomes a useful resource for people
- Builds a community at work
- Does not try to hold on to territory or turf
- Lets go of ego
- Creates a place in which people can find meaning in their work

Constructivist leaders are committed to service to others, not control of others; they view their role as a resource for people. These leaders serve others and respond to a problem by listening first. As in the prayer of Saint Francis, they "may not seek so much to be understood as to understand." They accept (never reject) what those around them offer, and they empathize with the feelings of others. They try to build a community at work. This type of behavior of the leader elicits trust, and followers freely respond because their leader is a proven and trusted servant. Constructivist leaders also do not try to hold on to their own territory (i.e., turf). Rather, they let go of their own egos. Finally, constructivist leaders create a place in which people can find meaning in their work.

All of these behaviors collectively describe the actions of the "servant as leader" (Greenleaf, 1977, p. 21). That is, the servant as leader—or, put more briefly, the servant-leader—listens first to others, accepts what others have to offer, empathizes with their feelings, and elicits trust. Greenleaf theorizes that caring and compassion for people is the rock upon which a good organization is built. He extends this theory with the following unequivocal corollary:

The only sound basis for trust is for people to have the solid experience of being *served* by their institutions in a way that builds a society that is more just and more loving, and with creative opportunities for all of its people. (p. 83)

The constructivist approach to leadership is clear in the servant-leader's view of the work given to members of the organization. Greenleaf (1977) states,

The work exists for the person as much as the person exists for the work. Put another way, the business exists as much to provide meaningful work to the person as it exists to provide a product or service to the customer. . . . The business then becomes a serving institution— serving those who produce and those who use. (pp. 154–155)

The constructivist leader desires to construct new knowledge on the building blocks of her followers' experiences. Thus, this leader understands the importance of creating and assigning meaningful and engaging work for her followers, whether that work is in the context of a staff development setting or the classroom. Finally, the constructivist leader understands that she must model constructivism in a staff development setting if teacher-followers are to integrate a constructivist approach into their classrooms.

> **Focus Group Response**
>
> "The key word here is 'servant'; the leader would be as willing to give as to receive."

Evidence of servant-leadership in any of Roosevelt's leaders can be seen in the operation of its SIT, building leadership team, or executive teachers. At such meetings, the prepared agenda reflects activities (i.e., learning experiences) that enable the learner to become involved in his or her own learning. Although the agenda is preset, the servant-leader enables flexibility to maximize the impact of the inservice goals and objectives. Reflection and dialogue are an important part of the learning and time on task. Goals of school improvement and building leadership are accomplished in a climate of openness, trust, professionalism, and empathy for each other.

> **Focus Group Response**
>
> "Staff meetings would be different. There would be continuous, active participation of teachers. Meetings would not be sitting and listening to information."
>
> "The leader would provide opportunities for growth; he would remove roadblocks, provide time, and ask compelling questions."

*Virtue 2: Individualized Consideration
(Supports Empowering Relationships)*

The virtue of Individualized Consideration is related to the Humane Dimension's second component, namely, Empowering Relationships. Evidence of this virtue may be found in the following behaviors of the constructivist leader, all of which are identified in Avolio and Bass's (2002) work on transformational leadership:

- Practices *management by walking around*
- Listens effectively
- Delegates as a means of developing followers
- Acts as a coach or mentor
- Creates new learning opportunities for followers
- Recognizes and accepts individual differences

Constructivist leaders are focused on the individual follower's needs and interests. To this end, the leader practices *management by walking around* to listen effectively to what others have to say. On the basis of needs and interests, the leader delegates as a means of developing followers. In this way, followers empower themselves to grow while the leader simply coaches by creating new learning opportunities through questioning, challenging, and supporting the individual follower's goals. Finally, the constructivist leader recognizes and accepts individual differences among followers.

> **Focus Group Response**
>
> "Listen. Trust."
>
> "Administrators would see that their primary job is to take down barriers so teachers can do what needs to be done. Administrators would ask, 'How can I help?'"

The key to empowering relationships is that each teacher—or administrator, for that matter—empowers himself or herself to grow. A leader's role in this empowerment process simply is to coach and support the follower. To further develop the follower's growth, the leader delegates on the basis of needs, interests, and strengths, and thus creates new learning opportunities for followers. Sergiovanni's (1994) comprehensive and exhaustive discussion on building professional learning communities in schools underpins the virtue of Individual Consideration and the Humane Dimension's second component, Empowering Relationships.

The principal means for empowering one's self is inquiry. Inquiry that reflects on practice and the search for solutions to teaching-and-learning problems is ultimately the only means to personal and professional growth. In the final analysis, only individuals may empower themselves to be the most efficacious leader in the classroom or organization at large. Sergiovanni (1994) summarizes this concept:

A commitment to exemplary practice means staying abreast of new developments, researching one's practice, and trying out new ideas. In a sense, it means accepting responsibility not only for one's own present practice but also for enhancing one's future practice through professional development. (p. 142)

As teachers, we stress inquiry-based learning with our students, and so we should stress the same mode of learning for ourselves. Inquiry-based staff development means introspective self-reflection, engagement in discourse with others, and overall school improvement through an examination of our own practices. Stated differently by Rearick and Feldman (1999), inquiry and reflection are of three types: autobiographical reflection, collaborative reflection, and communal reflection. Together, these three types of inquiry and reflection mirror the progression of Personal Transformation to Group Transformation to Organizational Transformation. Self-evidently, autobiographical reflection is more personal and introspective, whereas collaborative reflection extends to others' involvement in one's search for answers to teaching-and-learning questions. Finally, communal reflection suggests interaction in larger group situations.

When teacher efficacy is examined in a "culture of collaboration" (Fullan, 1993), a healthy, professional dissonance may be created because each other's ideas and values may conflict. That is, individuals are required to examine and reexamine their own assumptions about theory and practice. The questioning that results is what Lord (1994) refers to as productive disequilibrium. In a professional learning community, Individualized Consideration and empowerment confront group differences of perspectives until equilibrium and consonance are reached through collegial dialogue, reflection, and teamwork. Until that point is reached, the culture is in a temporary state of transformation, which Hackney, Reading, and Runnestrand (2000) call "a dangerous task" (p. 6) where existing value systems are being challenged.

> **Focus Group Response**
>
> "Evaluations would be different: not checklists, but conversations about goals and the help that is needed. Help would be ongoing."

Evidence of Individualized Consideration is clear in a district process of staff development that supports members' development of their own Individual Professional Development Plans (IPDPs). In a sense, an IPDP is a form of action research. A professional's wondering is transformed into a detailed study of local practice that ultimately is evaluated and documented as local knowledge (Cochran-Smith & Lytle, 1993).

An IPDP process should include opportunities for teachers to come together as persons with intense commitments to each other's growth (Greene, 1991). Stated differently, "A commitment to exemplary practice translates into a commitment to make the school a learning and inquiring community" (Sergiovanni, 1994, p. 143) where individual professional growth contributes to the group's growth as well.

Virtue 3: Idealized Leadership (Supports Other-Centered Purpose)

The virtue of Idealized Leadership is related to the Humane Dimension's third component, namely, Other-Centered Purpose. Evidence of this virtue may be found in the following behaviors of the constructivist leader, all of which are identified in Avolio and Bass's (2002) work on transformational leadership:

- Behaves as a role model for followers
- Considers the needs of others over own personal needs
- Shares risks with followers
- Can be counted on to do the right thing for others
- Avoids using power for personal gain
- Uses power only when needed

Constructivist leaders are focused on others, not self. The respect of leaders for their followers engenders the importance of their behavior as a role model, and so this leader shuns any actions that would result in her own self-satisfaction at the expense of others' satisfaction. In short, she considers the needs of others over personal needs. The leader's focus on others' goals and objectives leads her to share risks with followers as they pursue their goals. This leader can be counted on to do the right thing for others, and she especially avoids using power for personal gain. In fact, this leader uses power and authority only when needed.

Perhaps one of the best examples of other-centeredness among adults in the teaching profession is the cognitive coaching model of Costa and Garmston (1994). In the relationship between the leader as coach and the teacher as follower, all of the attention is focused on the teacher. Yet the teacher (i.e., the follower) is leading in every step along the way of the coaching process. Consider some of the steps outlined by Costa and Garmston: (a) the teacher determines what the coach should look for (i.e., in the teacher's classroom) and what feedback would

> **Focus Group Response**
>
> "Decisions are made in a dialogue process in which information is gathered from both teachers and administrators."

be desired and helpful; (b) the data collected by the coach are given to the teacher for self-analysis; (c) the teacher evaluates his or her own performance according to goals and criteria established by the teacher; and (d) the power to coach is bestowed by the teacher (i.e., teachers "allow" themselves to be coached because of the helpfulness and other-centeredness of their coach).

Evidence of idealized leadership is found in any school where a collegial climate of peer coaching or cognitive coaching (Costa & Garmston, 1994) exists. Thus, other-centeredness of the coaching model is the modus operandi in such a district. It is likely that not just the teacher (i.e., the follower) is transformed by the coaching process. Rather, the supervisor (i.e., the leader) also may be transformed as a result of this process. When the teachers and supervisors are transformed through the coaching model, the organization as a whole is transformed to support other-centeredness. So, the focus of the teacher is the student, and the focus of the leader is the teacher.

Virtue 4: Intellectual Stimulation (Supports Personal Transformation)

The virtue of Intellectual Stimulation is related to the Humane Dimension's fourth component, namely, Personal Transformation. Evidence of this virtue may be found in the following behaviors of the constructivist leader, all of which are identified in Avolio and Bass's (2002) work on transformational leadership:

- Stimulates followers' efforts to be innovative and creative
- Questions assumptions
- Reframes problems
- Approaches old situations in new ways
- Does not publicly criticize followers for their mistakes
- Solicits new ideas and creative problem solving
- Encourages followers to try new approaches
- Does not criticize ideas that are different from his or hers

Constructivist leaders "stimulate their followers' efforts to be innovative and creative by questioning assumptions, reframing problems, and approaching old situations in new ways" (Avolio & Bass, 2002, p. 2). When teachers and administrators question their assumptions and reframe their problems, they are more capable of embracing others' perspectives and professional practices and less capable of criticizing followers' mistakes and ideas. They are more prone to accept subjectivity, indefiniteness, ambiguity, vagueness, and abstraction in their lives and to solicit new ideas and new approaches. They do not accept any propensity to accept only definiteness, precision, and empirical "hard facts" in the world around them, even though this propensity could derive from the nature of physical science and its inevitable presence in all of our lives (Baatz, 1980).

The teacher's and leader's choices of teaching tools and methods are based on her own perspectives and assumptions about the world around her. We observe here two examples of the virtue of intellectual stimulation: in the constructivist classroom and in a constructivist leadership situation.

Evidence of constructivist teaching practices exists when a teacher seizes the opportunity of students' erroneous thinking and uses it as a "teachable moment." Observe a primary elementary science class where some students ask their teacher a question about the constantly decreasing level of water in the classroom's aquarium. They ask, "Are the fish drinking up the water?" The constructivist teacher finds a teachable moment here: The teacher and students proceed to conduct an experiment for the next two weeks with two different fish bowls. One bowl contains several goldfish, while the other bowl contains uninhabited water. But both bowls are filled originally to the same level. Obviously, both bowls will lose a similar amount of water in a two-week period. As a result, at the end of the two weeks, the teacher and students are more ready to discuss the concepts of evaporation, gas, and liquid. Now the students have seen that the fish are not "drinking up the water."

Evidence of intellectual stimulation in the leader's staff development room may be observed in an exemplary mentor/entry-year, teacher-training program, where collegiality prevails through practices of dialogue, reflection, journaling, and inquiry. In such programs, monthly meetings hardly are considered training sessions or lectures. Rather, inquiry and discovery prevail in a climate of professional exchanges and collaborative deliberations between mentors and new, entry-year teachers. Also, in these meetings are exchanged teachers' stories, journals, and narratives about the past month's events and critical events.

Further, evidence is found in the types of interactions taking place at this mentor meeting. Collaborative methods of participant-to-participant problem solving include mutual inquiry and discovery and probing questions that go beyond the knowledge level of Bloom's (1956) *Taxonomy of Educational Objectives.* That is, comprehension, application, analysis, synthesis, and evaluation are all levels of understanding in the taxonomy that become goals of the professional development in question. Along with these levels of understanding is likely to come a new knowledge based on the social construction of meaning from prior experiences of the adult learner.

In closing, although the constructivist leader brings all four virtues to the situation as one amorphous whole, application of the virtues is a cyclical concept. That is, the Humane Dimension grows in an organization as the leader develops Communications Based on Trust, Empowering Relationships, Other-Centered Purposes, and Personal and Organizational Transformation.

Focus Group Response

"There would be different organizational structures for decision making throughout the district."

Although the Humane Dimension is not necessarily and always a strict, linear model, its cycle of growth is a pattern of behaviors that is likely to occur in a predictable way.

ELEMENT 3: PARTICIPATORY LEADERSHIP STRUCTURES

Past Problems

It could be that there is no term in leadership and management literature that is more misunderstood or misused than "participatory management." Furthermore, there probably is no other term with as many alternate names, in spite of technically different meanings implied by each of these names. For example, *participatory management* and *shared decision making* could mean different things, even though both terms often are used interchangeably. Also, implications of participatory management often are equated to those of *site-based decision making*, but implications of each of these terms could vary in different contexts. The list could continue with many more examples.

Perhaps the main reason why participatory management has not disappeared totally from our psyche is found in this question: What would be the alternative to organizational members' participating in decision making? Consider the opposite of participative processes: the absence of participation, or autocracy.

> ### Focus Group Response
>
> "My participation in decision making must be genuine; that is, decisions are not already made. Honesty is important."

Unfortunately, participatory management has become a far more commonly used term than it has become a thoughtfully and effectively implemented practice in organizations. One often hears the apathetic response from organizational leaders "We tried that already; it didn't work!"

Present Promise

Rather than lamenting any further, we break ranks from our colleagues who are apathetic about this concept. (Some may say that "we did that in the 1980s." Perhaps the amount of literature on it has diminished in recent years, but there is no evidence that it cannot be used as a tool for decision making in today's schools.) We begin by recommending a more accurate term: *participatory leadership structures.* We choose this term for many reasons. The reader may recall our earlier discussion on leading versus managing, based on Kotter's (1996) work (see Chapter 1). Whether it is participatory or not, management is a concept better relegated to the

Managerial Domain; however, participatory leadership implies the commitment of a leader to operate in the Humane Dimension. Finally, the term *participatory leadership structures* implies multiple tools available to the leader. Further explanation is necessary here.

If leaders truly desire a high degree of participation, they must be open to the input of all others who are willing to be engaged in a process designed to arrive at group decisions. A process that works effectively in southern Ohio may not work in exactly the same way as it would in, say, southern Colorado. This contrast of process possibilities exists because, of course, cultures and groups may differ from one organization to another.

> **Focus Group Response**
>
> "Some of the confusion and mistrust comes about because we do not know what is done with our input. Even if the final decision does not align with mine, I would like to know how my ideas were used."

Yet the literature is replete with "cookbook" approaches to participatory management. (The reader is challenged to type this term in any Internet search engine. When we recently did so, the Internet generated 355,000 links!) The implication by too many writers is that an organization need only follow a recipe of procedures to cook up participatory management for its employees, and then all will feast on the benefits of collegiality and shared decision making. This cookbook approach is only part of the problem of a stale and trite image of participatory management in school districts.

Two other main problems have occurred during the past few decades when participatory management was introduced to school districts. First, it often was sold to employees as a "false bill of goods" that allegedly had the potential to single-handedly reform schools. That is, it was sold as a budgeting system that decentralized decisions in such a way that schools supposedly would be transformed (Giancola, 1988). Of course, participatory management never could meet the high expectations that were generated by managers when this "bandwagon rolled into town." Second, the managers who espoused the many benefits of participatory management never could let go of their position power long enough to encourage others (i.e., followers) to empower themselves with the freedom to make decisions, which could be beneficial for students and, at the same time, congruent with organizational goals. In short, traditional managers were being asked to become leaders without sufficient training to shift their mind-sets.

Nevertheless, success stories of participatory leadership structures are still found in schools. For example, Deal and Peterson (1999) write of Anna M. Joyce Elementary School in Detroit; they state, "Joyce gained control over its budget. It became more responsible for ensuring that resources were used to support the school's mission" (p. 109). The authors discuss this budgeting system in the context of shared decision making, another term for participatory leadership structures.

A Generic Model of Participatory Leadership Structures

We suggest a different but necessary approach to bring participatory leadership structures to one's organization. Not to ignore the many useful recommendations in the literature on participatory management and site-based decision making (e.g., Candoli, 1991; Chapman, 1990; Halliman, 1995; Herman & Herman, 1993; Murphy, 1995; Murphy & Beck, 1995; Wegenke, 1994), we turn to a generic model of participatory leadership structures. This generic model reflects an integration of five participatory management systems studied in detail during a two-year period (Giancola, 1988).

The generic model of participatory leadership structures is a system of seven subsystems that must interact dynamically in any locally developed model. (We stress that details of the model must be developed locally by stakeholders in the process. Literature sources such as those cited previously could provide a good starting point for leaders.) The seven subsystems and their brief descriptions are listed here:

Decision-Making Structure. This subsystem's function is to establish the leadership channels that organizational participants must use to provide input through representative leaders. Overall, the leadership channels must be distributed throughout the organization in such a manner that supports autonomy of decisions and operations but that does not ignore organizational goals.

Fiscal Responsibility. This subsystem's function is to assure that the funding that follows all decisions is reviewed with adequate checks and balances to protect public funds. These checks and balances must include accountability measures, regular financial reviews, and financial projections to anticipate needs.

School Budget Procedures. This subsystem's function is to outline activities to be used by representative leaders to gather and forward input from all stakeholders so that final budgets reflect the spending needs of organizational members. Barring unforeseen emergencies, all expenditures should be carried out in a planned program of expenditures.

Participant Involvement. This subsystem's function is to ensure that all stakeholders have an opportunity for involvement. Time must be allotted for organizational members to participate. The expected outcome of their participation is ownership of final decisions and expenditures. Also, the community at large must have an opportunity to become involved in some way.

Participant Perspectives. This subsystem's function is to provide a process for reviewing participant attitudes in a regular loop of information flow. The objective of this review is to build positive relations and understanding between organizational participants. Without a loop of feedback, misunderstandings occur.

Participant Learning Processes. This subsystem's function is to provide the staff development necessary for efficient and effective participation by all stakeholders. Training must be comprehensive and must cover all other subsystems in the entire model. Printed materials should be emphasized as a means of documenting all details of the model. Direct experience in the staff development program must be required, although vicarious experience through representative leaders may be necessary to increase efficiency of the model.

> **Focus Group Response**
>
> "It seems to me there is some distrust when your opinion is asked for and then is disregarded. That is insulting, disrespectful."

Educational Impact. This subsystem's function is to assure the connection of all educational and financial decisions to the students' education. Classroom curriculum and instruction must be the primary focus of all stakeholders. In addition, school climate and facilities must be the secondary focus of all stakeholders.

These seven subsystems of the generic model of participatory leadership structures form the backbone of any participatory management system. Since we have been using this rubric in meta-analyses of such systems, we have yet to uncover any bit of information related to participatory management that does not fit into one of the subsystems. Based on research, this generic model provides organizational leaders with a framework for decision making and budgeting that offers a required alternative to autocracy in the Humane Dimension.

At Roosevelt High School, all seven subsystems are evident to any observer searching for these leadership structures in practice. Though not formally defined in notebooks on each staff member's bookshelf, these seven subsystems have become part of the school's leadership culture.

ELEMENT 4: WIN/WIN CONSENSUS BUILDING, NEGOTIATING, AND DECISION MAKING

Looking back at the first three elements of our transformed leadership culture, we believe not only that a fourth element is missing but also that it is required for organizational transformation to occur: win/win consensus building, negotiating, and decision making. In short, "both sides win" (i.e., such is the origin of the term win/win) when consensus is achieved rather than when compromise is reached. Both sides win when bilateral negotiations are based on a win/win process rather than a traditional proposal-counterproposal bargaining model. And both sides win when a decision is documented and reviewed through dialogue sessions subsequent to the negotiations.

We remind the reader that a transformed leadership culture begins with a true team, bonded together by constructivist virtues and operating in a system of participatory leadership structures or subsystems. But this cycle of cultural growth is not complete until both cultures of teachers and administrators, respectively, can reach decisions mutually arrived at by a win/win process of consensus building, negotiating, and decision making.

Win/Win's Three Steps

A win/win process has three steps. The first step is that participants agree to a consensus-building, not compromise-reaching, method of problem solving. The second step is that actual win/win negotiations are used in place of a traditional proposal-counterproposal bargaining model. (We pause here to ask the reader to imagine a bargaining table where all participants in the process come ready to exchange ideas, issues, and concerns in an open and trusting environment unfettered with historical obstacles from the past. In contrast, consider the traditional proposal-counterproposal model in which two sides come to the table with their "minds already made up"!) The third step is that final decisions are documented and reviewed through regular dialogue sessions after negotiations. What follows is an elaboration of these three steps.

Win/Win Step 1: Consensus Building, Not Compromise Reaching

First, a consensus-building, not compromise-reaching, method of problem solving must be discussed, bought into, and used consistently by all stakeholders of a decision. We return to the work of Follett (1924), whom we cited in Chapter 1. More than 75 years ago, she attacked the traditional proposal-counterproposal bargaining model on the basis of its dependence on *compromise.*

When two parties taking sides in an argument compromise, each one loses a piece of ownership in the final resolution. That is, the extent to which one gives up any bit of self-interest is the degree of ownership lost in the solution.

In place of compromise, Follett (1924) encourages the creative experience of *consensus building* as the means to resolve problems in an organization. Ultimately, a shared decision, goal, or vision is one in which individuals integrate their ideas into a new and creative idea yet to be submitted (i.e., in place of the inertia that occurs when each individual is predisposed to his or her own idea). In the process of *integration,* Follett (1924) espouses that opinions of people involved in group decision making are shaped by the process itself. Specifically, each person involved in the process influences the thinking of others, so that the final product or decision is not merely the sum of the individual contributions but rather something new and different from that sum. That is, personal transformation will have occurred. Thus, the final decision is a new and creative solution, or integration, resulting from consensus, not compromise. She notes that with compromise, each participant gives up a piece of his or her viewpoint to move the decision along; this is not the case with consensus. In short, everyone can and does win.

We also look at the work of Argyris (1999b) to add value to consensus building. Only during this kind of authentic and truthful dialogue is there hope that individuals will not hold back with the worry that what they say could be problematic for them. He describes this worry when he states, "Individuals deal with embarrassment or threat with another set of skillful—hence tacit—actions. . . . These actions are counterproductive to effective management" (p. 123). Through consensus building, we believe that such tacit actions will be minimized.

> **Focus Group Response**
>
> "This takes time and personal integrity. It also takes a willingness to consider or commit to a win/win, third solution."

Win/Win Step 2: Negotiating

The second step of win/win is that a consensus-building process is used in negotiations in place of a traditional proposal-counterproposal bargaining model. Although many proprietary sources of procedures for win/win negotiations may exist in the literature and on the Internet, we recommend here a generic process of procedures for win/win negotiations, originally designed by Crisci and Herpel (1984).

The generic process may be summarized in terms of the following six sessions and their goals:

> **Focus Group Response**
>
> "Leaders have to model a willingness to go after an alternative solution."

1. First session: Selection of an experienced win/win facilitator

2. Second session: Initial planning meeting

3. Third session: Information sharing

4. Fourth session: Prioritizing questions, issues, and concerns

5. Fifth session: Addressing questions, issues, and concerns (may be repeated)

6. Final session (after multiple fifth sessions): Final agreement

(A rich description and elaboration of each session previously described is found in Resource F.)

Win/Win Step 3: Decision Making and Reviewing Through Dialogue Sessions

In the traditional proposal-counterproposal bargaining model, the conventional method of correcting any problems that arise from the implementation of a new contract is the informal and formal steps of the negotiated grievance procedure. With the win/win process of negotiations, an additional process is added to prevent the use of the grievance procedure or even unfair labor practices as a means of resolving conflicts. This additional process is the communications forum referred to as ongoing dialogue sessions.

> **Focus Group Response**
>
> "More input and expertise are brought out in win/win. An outside facilitator may be needed to be sure that every voice is heard."

Reasons for the use of dialogue sessions include the following: resolution of matters deferred at the collective-bargaining table to dialogue sessions, clarification of any matters related to implementing new contract language (i.e., in lieu of the grievance procedure as a clarifying process), and a forum for addressing new issues and concerns that arise. These reasons must form the basis for specific design details of a framework that is acceptable to all stakeholders.

The framework for dialogue sessions should be developed by a subcommittee, representative of members from both sides of the original bargaining teams. Details of the framework must not exclude lessons learned from the win/win bargaining process. At the very least, the initial planning meeting's orientation on the nature of win/win, its solutions, and consensus building must become the foundation of future dialogue sessions, unless of course the original negotiations reverted back to a traditional proposal-counterproposal bargaining model before the win/win contract negotiations were completed. (The reader should recall that with win/win negotiations, *voluntary participation* is emphasized, and either side understands that it has the right to withdraw from the process at any time and to return to conventional bargaining should a team's members become dissatisfied with win/win negotiations.)

With the establishment of periodic dialogue sessions, preferably facilitated by the original facilitator and cofacilitator, not only contract issues will be addressed before they become problems. Rather, general personnel issues and practices also will be improved through a framework designed to improve communication and collaboration.

Although the administration and staff of Roosevelt High School do not negotiate directly for wages and benefits, these professionals do demonstrate win/win procedures in many of their ongoing decision-making structures (e.g., executive teacher, building technology, and appreciative inquiry evaluation committees). The district's board office administrators are the ones responsible for negotiating all wages, terms, and conditions of employment. However, during board-office negotiations with the Kent Educators Association (KEA), most elements of win/win have been used to address interests and concerns of both sides.

> **Focus Group Response**
>
> "A win/win mentality assumes that the old way must be scrapped. People have to be open to creative brainstorming so that they do not fall back on what they have always done in the past. They have to be open to new possibilities going into deliberations."

APPLYING THE HUMANE DIMENSION

Specific staff development activities for incorporating the elements of a transformed leadership culture are essentially the same as those activities listed in Resources A, B, C, and D. That is, activities for developing the Humane Dimension's components are the main focus of our work, which eventually leads to transformed organizational cultures. However, we do recognize the need to recommend some specific activities from our notebooks of Professional Development Notepad exercises that specifically relate to the four elements of both the Transformed Leadership Culture and the Transformed Teacher Culture. The following exercises are offered as only a beginning to understanding the infrastructure of these two cultures.

ELEMENT 1 EXERCISE

Team First/Vision Later

One easy exercise for building team is to increase members' knowledge about each other's families. Personal conversations on this topic of family may dig deeply into the hearts of individuals engaged in this dialogue. Follow these four steps:

1. At the beginning of a meeting, each individual is given a blank sheet with a list of personal questions, such as place of birth, place of spouse's or partner's birth, spouse's or partner's name, number and ages of any children, siblings' names, and so on.

2. The number of questions should be twice the number of participants in the group.

3. Each member must circulate for 15 minutes among other members of the group until two questions per member are answered.

4. After the exercise, each member shares with the whole group interesting facts about their team.

ELEMENT 2 EXERCISE

Constructivist Practices for Administrators

A leader's interest in supporting the growth of staff members begins with understanding others' most pressing, professional needs or concerns. Collegial sharing of these concerns increases understanding and capacity to address these concerns. Follow these six steps:

1. At a staff meeting, the leader breaks up the group into pairs.

2. Each member of the pair has five minutes to share with the other a professional concern about a personally troublesome area of instruction or of a lesson.

3. The other member of the pair has five minutes to respond with nonjudgmental questions about how and why the concern exists, and what might be done to improve that area.

4. Examples of such questions might be: Have you tried _____ (suggestion)? or What would happen if _____ (action)?

5. Responses to these questions are recorded by the pairs.

6. The leader invites any staff member who is interested to share concerns and these responses at the next evaluation conference.

ELEMENT 3 EXERCISE

Participatory Leadership Structures

Participant learning processes are an important function in site-based decision making (SBDM). In addition to intensive training sessions, regular staff may be used to develop understanding of participatory leadership. Follow these six steps:

1. At an administrative team meeting or teacher-staff meeting, the leader asks all participants to share elements or components they think should exist in SBDM.

2. A recorder writes these items on chart paper.

3. A completed page of chart paper is separated from the pad and hung on the wall.

4. This process continues until a saturation point in the discussion occurs.

5. An overhead is used to show the seven subsystems of a generic model of participatory leadership.

6. Each item on the chart paper is evaluated and related to one of the seven subsystems. At the end, the items are described as the possible beginning of that organization's SBDM.

ELEMENT 4 EXERCISE

*Win/Win Consensus Building,
Negotiating, and Decision Making*

To build understanding of win/win techniques, members of a group must develop a sense of how a unique and creative solution to a problem may exist. The following five steps are a simple exercise that helps the staff to understand creative problem solving:

1. The large group should be divided into small groups of about four members.

2. Each small group is given a sheet of paper with a problem written on it (e.g., The length of a building's monthly staff meeting recently

has become a topic of debate because of the many personal issues and commitments that need attention after work; morning meetings have the same potential for a problem. Develop a solution to this problem.).

3. Using chart paper, the small group's recorder writes down every suggested solution that is generated during a brainstorming session.

4. Suggestions that have no negative impact on any member of the small group are identified.

5. Consensus on which suggestion to use finally is determined.

REFLECTION

As you proceed through the next chapter on the Transformed Teacher Culture, reflect after reading about each element on how you might incorporate your new knowledge into staff development opportunities and into your own life.

Elements of a Transformed Teacher Culture

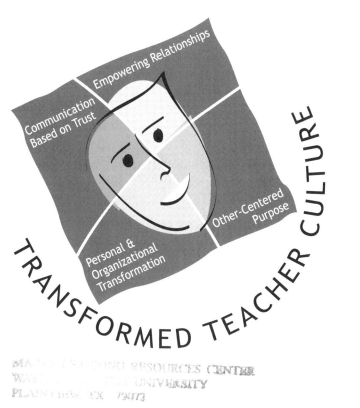

Like the elements of the transformed leadership culture, the elements of this chapter have been observed during our work at Roosevelt High School, and our discovery of them emerged from the final results of the appreciative inquiry process (Cooperrider & Whitney, 1999). Staff members reflected on what made their school environment so positive. Their discussion of relationships between the staff at all levels, students, and parents corroborated our conclusion of the Humane Dimension's capacity to connect layers of people to each other.

The rationale underlying the creation of a Humane Dimension is to connect the potentially separated cultures of teachers and administrators. It is our firm belief that until these two groups of educators work more closely with each other to support their shared beliefs, the possibility exists for teachers to work and develop in one culture while principals and other administrators work and try to lead in another. The image that comes to mind is two young children in "parallel play." Both children may be having a wonderful time and, one supposes, accomplishing a great deal, but the wonder and accomplishments are magnified when the two come together. For school transformation to be both wonderful and productive, the best of both cultures must be united. The best, or ideal, teacher culture will likely differ from the traditional teacher culture.

The traditional teacher culture can be characterized by a number of traits, including hierarchical conceptions of leadership, speaker-driven staff development approaches, a separation of curriculum and instruction, and nonformative appraisal systems. What would a teacher's world look like in a place where **Communication is Based on Trust, Other-Centered Purpose** prevails, people are **Empowered** through their **Relationships** with each other, and **Personal Transformation** is expected? This place, it should be clear by now, is the *Humane Dimension*. As this dimension continues to expand in a school, we have observed a transformed teacher culture characterized by the following elements:

- Nontraditional conceptions of leadership
- Constructivist practices for teachers
- Curriculum-driven staff development
- Appraisal systems designed for a culture of professional worth

ELEMENT 1: NONTRADITIONAL CONCEPTIONS OF LEADERSHIP

Educational leadership, according to Maxcy (1991), is "often confused with administration" (p. 77). This confusion, as explained in Chapter 3 on "Empowering Relationships," poses a problem for educational reform. In an insightful piece on teacher leadership and school reform, Fullan (1994) explains that there is no chance for serious education reform until the

conception of teacher leadership is expanded. Fullan offers two fundamental reasons for the profession's limited conception of teacher leadership. He maintains, first, that "despite the rhetoric about teacher education
in today's society, there does not seem to be a real belief or confidence that
investing in teacher development will get results" (p. 241) and, second,
"the strategies for teacher leadership that are used are superficial" (p. 241).
To achieve a conception of teacher leadership that will (a) be for all
teachers and (b) lead to serious education reform, Fullan proposes a broader,
more thoughtful conception of teacher leadership.

Thoughtful Conceptions of Teacher Leadership

Not only, as Fullan (1994) claims, are the strategies used for teacher
leadership superficial, we argue that many educators see through the limited amount of position power available to a relatively small number of
teachers. As Fullan and Hargreaves (1996) put it, these "[n]ew roles can be
superficial, contrived, overly bureaucratic" (p. 12). Traditionally, opportunities for teachers to lead are allotted to roles such as department chair,
team leader, or mentor. Teacher leaders who assume these roles have limited decision-making authority. Typically, these individuals function in
an advisory capacity to administrators who do make the decisions. In
essence, then, what we have in our schools is not so much teacher leadership as it is teacher involvement in activities outside the classroom.
Teachers should be involved in activities outside the classroom, particularly those that have to do with curriculum and instruction. Yet our schools
are structured in ways that reward educators who leave the classroom
to take on administrative roles. The people who leave the classroom and
go into administration are given higher salaries (because of additional
responsibilities and a greater number of annual work days) and more discretionary time than those who choose to remain in the classroom with
students. This statement is not meant to take away from the critical work
that school administrators do. It is, however, meant to demonstrate the
unequal distribution of leadership opportunities, responsibilities, and,
therefore, power in our schools.

Fullan and Hargreaves (1996) argue
that "when responsibility is left solely
to formal leaders, it overloads them,
resulting in incorrect and frequently
imposed solutions" (p. 12). Teachers,
who greatly outnumber principals in
their buildings, can perpetuate both the
hierarchy and the burden on administra-
tors by their expectation to be led. Lambert, Collay, Dietz, Kent, and
Richert (1996) illustrate this by explaining that "when teachers take action
outside their classroom only when authorized, when they wait for

> **Focus Group Response**
>
> "Divide the power, and divide the responsibilities."
>
> "Teach people to lead."

permission to be innovators, they are signaling that an adult-to-adult relationship is not expected" (p. 30). Thus, the opportunity for an Empowering Relationship is lost.

School transformation, we have argued throughout this book, begins with the personal transformation of the individual. Lambert et al. (1996) cite Peter Block (1993) in his work on stewardship: "If there is not transformation inside us, all the structural change in the world will have no impact on our institutions" (p. 72). Before teachers and administrators can begin to enact thoughtful conceptions of teacher leadership, individual educators will have to change their expectations about who should do what in our schools. Deep change, write Fullan and Hargreaves (1996),

> involves broadening the conception of the teacher so that individual teachers bring even more resources to bear on the classroom as a result of being routinely connected to a larger web of professional deliberations. Teacher leadership, defined as the capacity and commitment to contribute beyond one's own classroom, should be valued and practiced from the beginning to the end of every teacher's career. There are few more basic things to fight for. (pp. 12–13)

Lambert et al. (1996) agree with both the definition of teacher leadership and its importance. They write, "If leading is viewed as facilitating the learning of colleagues in a community, it becomes not only a feasible endeavor for teachers but a moral imperative" (p. 19). In the Humane Dimension, teacher leadership would have as an Other-Centered Purpose the goal of supporting the learning of other teachers in the building. To transcend a traditional notion of leadership, Communication Based on Trust is paramount. Empowering Relationships will help ensure expanding conceptions of teacher leadership that is not confined to set roles and predetermined responsibilities. Finally, genuine and meaningful teacher leadership can result when we shift from external, speaker-driven staff development to Personal Transformation. Teacher leadership within the Humane Dimension is the supporting of colleagues' personal transformation in relationships where learning is both reciprocal and interactive. Specific guidelines for building teacher leadership in our schools and in teacher education follow.

Guidelines for Teacher Leadership in Schools

Supporting Teacher Leadership

In order for teachers to support their colleagues' personal transformation, support for leadership roles and responsibilities is in order. The kind of support that teacher leaders need can run the gamut from simple to sophisticated. Simple forms of support would be those that require little time, money, and effort and limited planning and training. Examples of such simple forms of support for teacher leadership can include the following:

- Regularly scheduled released time for leadership activities
- Collaboration time built into the daily schedule
- Job-sharing opportunities
- District purchase of books for group study
- Stipends for afterschool or summer work

More sophisticated forms of support for teacher leadership may look like this:

- Every adult in the district who is certified or licensed to teach might teach at least one class each week. This would include administrators and counselors. Not only would this release full-time teachers to assume leadership responsibilities, it would increase the credibility of all faculty members by refocusing their efforts on student learning. Furthermore, the problems that can emerge from the unequal power relations in our schools could be greatly reduced.
- Collaborations between schools and universities should be strengthened to help design "teacher leadership cohorts" comprised of teachers, administrators, and university faculty. Their co-constructed curriculum could help bridge the current gap between educational administration departments and curriculum and instruction departments in most colleges of education.
- Professional evaluation designs should be redesigned to assess teacher development in more authentic, meaningful ways. A district committee of teacher association members and administrators would have to examine more nontraditional ways of assessing teacher performance.
- School calendars and schedules would have to be altered to provide the time needed for significant advances in teacher development.

Leadership Roles and Responsibilities

Support of a thoughtful and broader conception of teacher leadership has the potential for unlimited roles and responsibilities. What follows is only the beginning of what should be expanded within schools by teachers and administrators.

> **Focus Group Response**
>
> "Structures are built in for a variety of people to take on leadership roles."

Leadership Role 1: Study Group Leader. Because of the intense demands of planning, teaching, grading, and so on, classroom teachers can become "unread professionals." Student teachers and first-year teachers have been known to comment on this phenomenon to their university professors. Recently, in one of her graduate classes, Hutchison (1997) heard this from her student teachers and returning first-year teachers during a discussion about constructivism and best practice research. The returning teachers cautioned the novices that not everything they are studying will be evident or even welcomed in their schools. "Some veteran teachers," one class member remarked, "haven't read a book or a journal article in years."

> **Focus Group Response**
>
> "A district [leader] will make sure that those people who agree that leadership is not just a position are hired."

Several school districts have met this challenge of the unread professional by forming study groups around various topics such as assessment literacy and unit design. Because these topics are of primary importance to classroom instruction, teachers should lead the study groups. One or two teachers who have an interest in the topic could be given time to read materials and to plan a series of group study topics. The support for this leadership role is minimal yet necessary for the role to be taken seriously and to be perpetuated among the ranks of classroom teachers.

Leadership Role 2: Lesson Analyst. Teachers want to teach well, and teaching well begins with good planning that is enacted in the classroom. As teachers attempt to design lessons around new standards with an emphasis on student engagement, peers could provide a different and specific form of leadership. During the planning phase, a teacher leader could work with an individual teacher or with a small group of teachers (e.g., grade level) to assist in the writing of lesson objectives and design of delivery strategies. During the teaching phase, a teacher leader could observe the lesson of one teacher and give feedback after the class. This type of leadership offers assistance, not assessment, of teaching.

Leadership Role 3: Descriptive Review Partner. This leadership role could be used to assist classroom teachers in the analysis of student work or of student behavior. After an assignment has been completed, teachers could spend time with their descriptive review partners to discuss what the students have done. The conversation could focus on student engagement, mastery, or even needed interventions. If the topic in the review discussion is a particular student's behavior, the teacher would share in what ways the student is difficult to teach. The leader would help provide resources to address the difficulty (e.g., other teachers, support staff, instructional materials, specific interventions, etc.).

Leadership Role 4: Model Teacher. The mission statements of many schools convey specific instructional goals. For instance, a school's mission statement may focus on student literacy. Other schools may not articulate a specific statement about raising standardized test scores in certain subject areas, but the intent is there, all the same. These goals can be achieved with clarity and efficiency through teacher leadership. An elementary school with the aim of improving math test scores could use one primary teacher and one intermediate teacher to take the lead on this mission. Each teacher might be released for one or two hours from the classroom every day to conduct model math lessons for their peers. Additional responsibilities could include lesson observations and peer planning.

Leadership Role 5: Assessment Leaders. Standards-based education is changing how teachers use student assessment in their work. Rather than serving only as measurements *of* learning, assessments are more and more serving as measurements *for* learning. In other words, assessments are used to gather information about student learning while it is taking place and, therefore, to help modify instruction. This expanded understanding of assessment could be greatly enhanced with guidance from lead teachers. Assessment leaders could help their fellow classroom teachers design various assessments and analyze results. Instruction modifications that result could include re-teachings, interventions, material development, and so on.

Leadership Role 6: Action Research Advisors. Many educators are discovering the power of action research as a tool that links inquiry to improvement. Small-scale studies on teacher practices can be conducted on any number of topics such as classroom management, gender equity in the classroom, and specific strategy instruction such as note taking and study skills. A district could use the research expertise of one or two classroom teachers to lead the action research of groups of teachers. An action research advisor should be a teacher who has some advanced training in data collection (e.g., surveys, interviews, observations, documents, etc.) and data analysis. The advisor's responsibilities would include helping teachers construct researchable questions, providing literature resources, teaching the components of a literature review, helping collect data, and assisting in data analysis. Depending on the number of teacher researchers in a district, these tasks could be accomplished with a few hours of released time a week.

Leadership Role 7: Peer Evaluator. It is interesting to note the interest educators have in the topic of "authentic assessment" of student learning, yet when it comes to professional evaluations, there is little that is authentic or meaningful. A section that follows on a "Culture of Professional Worth" will provide greater detail about authentic professional assessments. Briefly stated here is a description of a teacher leader who conducts peer evaluations. This leader could take on the responsibility of assessing fellow teachers after training in instructional analysis and professional conferencing. Most building administrators would welcome assistance in a task that has grown time-consuming and, often, ineffective for promoting teacher growth. A peer evaluator would have to be a respected teacher who maintains some classroom teaching responsibilities. The peer evaluator would then have the credibility needed for realistic assessments to take place.

Leadership Role 8: Staff Development Designer and Facilitator. Staff development that works, according to Darling-Hammond and McLaughlin (1995), is connected to teachers' work with their students, linked to concrete tasks of teaching, organized around problem solving, and sustained over time by ongoing conversation and coaching (p. 598). The kind of staff development that will have the greatest impact on student learning requires a new form of leadership that cannot be facilitated by administrators alone. Teachers can be tapped to take the lead on any number of staff development initiatives. Every district has teachers who show interest in specific topics related to classroom practices. Ongoing training, research, and practice evidence this interest. These teachers can be "trained to train" and then be relieved of teaching duties all day or part of a day for one or two years. During this time, the leaders could design staff development sessions and follow-up that would meet the needs of teachers in that district.

Leadership Role 9: Peer Coach. Successful staff development is not limited to a workshop or a class. Ongoing support in the form of classroom observations and group discussions can help embed desired staff development goals. This kind of follow-up takes time and the kind of support that peer coaches provide. Some districts have successfully used peer coaches to observe teachers as they try out a new strategy and then give them feedback. Other districts use peer coaches to facilitate group discussions on practices.

Leadership Role 10: Mentor. Mentoring is a traditional teacher leader role, but too often this role has been a limited one because of the amount of time allotted to the functions of the role. Mentors should be viewed as resident scholars or master teachers. They should be released from teaching duties in some fashion to allow them to observe, confer, and counsel. This kind of support for the mentor would elevate the role to its true status of leader.

All of these teacher-leader roles have been derived from our observations at Roosevelt High School. Although not always formally planned or intended, these roles have been instrumental in transforming the teacher culture. We recommend, however, that these roles be formalized in a culture as much as possible to ensure systemic reform of that culture.

ELEMENT 2: CONSTRUCTIVIST PRACTICES FOR TEACHERS

Perhaps the most commonly shared attribute of current education reform initiatives is an embedded theory of constructivism. From the National Science Teachers Association's emphasis on learner-inquiry and hands-on experimentation to the National Council for Teachers of Mathematics' focus on student-generated questions and solutions, the dominant trend is clear: As a critical part of both curriculum and instructional design, constructivism has found its way into our classrooms. Yet as Fosnot notes in the Foreword to Brooks and Brooks's (1993) work that clearly defines constructivism, *The Case for the Constructivist Classroom*, "Constructivism is not a theory about teaching. It's a theory about knowledge and learning" (p. vii). The five guiding principles of a constructivist pedagogy are as follows:

1. *Posing problems of emerging relevance to students* requires a deep understanding of curriculum and a creative design of student work.

2. *Structuring learning around primary concepts:* The quest for essence suggests an organization of information and knowledge around conceptual clusters.

3. *Seeking and valuing students' points of view* helps make learning experiences both contextual and meaningful.

4. *Adapting curriculum to address students' suppositions* means that the students' reflective abstractions, perceptions, and interests must be considered when designing a learning experience.

5. *Assessing student learning in the context of teaching* requires a shift in the teacher's understanding of "assessment." Rather than serving merely as a measurement of learning, assessment is used to inform ongoing instruction. (Brooks & Brooks, 1993, pp. 35–98)

The academic content standards that are emerging from learned organizations of science, math, language arts, and other scholars directly reflect these five principles. Students are learning in ways that they may never have learned before, with the goal of "deep understanding, not imitative behavior" (Brooks & Brooks, 1993, p. 16). Deep understanding, not imitative behavior, should be the same worthy goal for teacher learning as well. Yet as Lieberman (1995) notes,

> what everyone appears to want for students—a wide array of learning opportunities that engage students in experiencing, creating, and solving real problems, using their own experiences, and working with others—is for some reason denied to teachers when

they are the learners. In the traditional view of staff development, workshops and conferences conducted outside the school count, but authentic opportunities to learn from and with colleagues *inside* the school do not. . . .

The ways teachers learn may be more like the ways students learn than we have previously recognized. Learning theorists and organizational theorists are teaching us that people learn best through active involvement and through thinking about and becoming articulate about what they have learned. (p. 592)

A constructivist view of teacher learning is a critical component of the Humane Dimension in that, as the five principles suggest, Communication and Empowerment enhance the growth and Personal Transformation of the individual. In a constructivist pedagogy, the teacher's purpose is to serve the learner's development, and the goal is personal transformation, or deep understanding, and not memorization or imitation. Contrast a constructivist view of staff development with a traditional view. Before the staff development event takes place, communication is typically limited to announcements of the latest workshop; during the training, communication is limited to teacher talk, with handouts, transparencies, and PowerPoint slides. Superficial rewards such as certificates, attendance hours, and stipends are substituted for true empowerment. The purpose of most of these sessions is to transmit information, and the goal is to have as many staff members trained as possible.

However, just as students are encouraged to construct their own deep understandings of important concepts in a constructivist classroom, teachers should be encouraged to do the same when it comes to their own professional development. As such, teachers are viewed as thinkers with emerging theories about their own teaching. In essence, then, teachers are the leaders of their own learning. The same four virtues of constructivist leaders are required of teachers in this role of leading their own learning. (See Chapter 6 for a detailed description of these four virtues.)

> ### Focus Group Response
>
> "When our 'inservice days' follow agendas structured without our input, I usually do not get as much out of the event."

The Virtues of Constructivist Professional Development

As teachers evolve throughout their careers, the ones who tend to stand out as models of lifelong learners typically have made many deliberate decisions about their own professional growth. These decisions are based on a desire to know more about an instructional strategy, a curriculum innovation, a pedagogical theory, and so on to meet the needs of their students. Parallelling the four virtues of the constructivist leader (see Chapter 3), the virtue that characterizes this behavior is servant-leadership (Greenleaf, 1977), which, according to Autry (2002), is evidenced by an individual who does the following:

- Becomes a useful resource for people
- Does not try to hold on to territory (or turf)
- Lets go of ego
- Creates a place in which people can find meaning in their work

Teachers who consciously take the lead in their own learning do so primarily for the sake of others. These others who are served by the individual teacher's professional growth are usually students but can be fellow educators as well. For example, student learning in a mixed-ability classroom certainly will be enhanced when the teacher becomes more knowledgeable about differentiated instruction. Individual students will be challenged and supported by this teacher's efforts to learn more about designing instructional activities and assessments for students who fall along a continuum of cognitive abilities. In the right environment, this teacher's peers could also benefit from this individual's professional development. Peers in the same grade level, team, or department could learn new strategies from this teacher in small-group discussions or classroom observations. Support personnel, such as special education tutors, could use this teacher's approaches as springboards for their own professional development.

The virtue of servant-leadership (Greenleaf, 1977) as it applies to a constructivist pedagogy of professional development is fostered in the right environment. In the wrong setting, an individual's development can be treated as a self-centered endeavor. Knowledge can be hoarded and instructional strategies hidden behind closed doors. Too often schools are the wrong places for teachers to view their own professional growth as a service to others. In the Humane Dimension, where Communication Based on Trust, Empowering Relationships, Other-Centered Purposes, and Personal and Organizational Transformation are continually expanding notions and events, the virtue of servant-leadership and individual professional development are deeply connected. One nourishes the other.

> **Focus Group Response**
>
> "Staff development would not be a one-time affair but, instead, would have follow-up like discussion groups, observations, or problem-solving groups."

Professional growth is equally enhanced by the second virtue of Individualized Consideration. Avolio and Bass (2002) provide a description of this virtue in their work on transformational leaders who do the following:

- Recognize and accept individual differences
- Act as a coach or mentor
- Create new learning opportunities for followers

Teachers who empower themselves to grow in the profession through ongoing reflection, study, reading, and so on take the lead in their own learning. In the Humane Dimension, the individual's professional confidence (and personal confidence, one hopes) grows within an environment of support and acceptance. Individual differences among teachers naturally exist because of the variety of teacher interests, abilities, responsibilities, roles, and personalities. Instead of mandating that *all* teachers in a building (or grade level or team) learn to design integrated curriculum units, those individual teachers who are interested in this topic might be given multiple opportunities to study integrated curriculum, project-based learning, unit design, and others. Professional development opportunities could include training, shared planning time, on-site visits, and materials. These teachers could then mentor other teachers who may begin to show interest in trying out their own integrated instructional units. Professional coaching could be a natural outgrowth of the conversations about shared practices among individual teachers. Professional coaching could then be an intermediate step between personal transformation and organizational transformation; we suggest that this intermediate step could be *group transformation.*

The third virtue of Idealized Leadership is directly related to a constructivist pedagogy of staff development. Teaching is a career that, almost by definition, has limited opportunities for advancement. The majority of educators who do not want to leave the classroom for positions in counseling, supervision, or administration can spend 30 to 40 years teaching students. For these individuals, there are limited numbers of leadership opportunities such as department chairs, team leaders, and mentors. When teachers take charge of their own learning, they can demonstrate key behaviors of constructivist leaders (Avolio & Bass, 2002):

> **Focus Group Response**
>
> "Professional development would be part of the normal rhythm of the day, not occur once a month. For example, grade-level or department teachers should be given the same lunch schedule to work together regularly."

- Behave as role models for followers
- Share risks with followers

Although ours is a time when scholarship is not widely honored (some say we exist in a culture of anti-intellectualism), the educational profession must put intellectual endeavors at the forefront. The educators we should honor with greater salary (for additional leadership responsibilities and longer formal work year) and discretionary time are not just the ones who leave the classroom for traditional leadership roles. When we begin to practice a constructivist pedagogy for professional development, one potential result could be innumerable leadership roles for teachers. Teachers can remain in the classroom and, at the same time, lead by being role models to other teachers. Peer observations could be "worth a thousand words" of a graduate lecture class. Peer coaching could be an expenditure of time and energy more valuable than consultant fees. And teachers could remain in the classroom where they want to be.

A constructivist pedagogy for staff development can be characterized by the fourth virtue of Intellectual Stimulation. According to Avolio and Bass (2002), this virtue can be seen in the behaviors of a leader who does the following:

- Stimulates followers' efforts to be innovative and creative
- Questions assumptions
- Reframes problems
- Approaches old situations in new ways
- Solicits new ideas and creative problem solving
- Encourages followers to try new approaches
- Does not criticize ideas that are different than his or hers

Imagine a school where teachers are supported in these ways. Teachers who are trying out portfolio assessment would be stimulated to be innovative and creative. They would be encouraged to voice their questions about students' contributions to their assessments. A group of teachers who are studying new ways of unit design would be given time to reframe the course of study in new ways. Two teachers who are studying an innovative approach to reading instruction would be asked to share their student work with other teachers in grade-level or faculty meetings. What these three scenarios share in common is the virtue of Intellectual Stimulation.

Practices and Policies That Promote a Constructivist Pedagogy of Staff Development

In 1996, the work of the National Commission on Teaching and America's Future resulted in a publication critical to any deliberation on school reform. The book, *What Matters Most: Teaching for America's Future* (National Commission on Teaching and America's Future, 1996),

> **Focus Group Response**
>
> "We do not always need administrators in our midst to develop professionally. I like to work with a partner in an ongoing fashion."

offers a startling comparison of teaching conditions in schools around the world and concludes with recommendations for supporting excellent teaching in all U.S. schools.

One comparison of teaching conditions focused on how countries invest in teachers (National Commission on Teaching and America's Future, 1996). In an analysis of educational staff by function, the United States is the only country, in comparison to Belgium, Japan, Italy, Australia, Finland, France, and Denmark, to spend less than half of its schools' budgets on teachers (about 43%). We spend nearly 27% on instructional staff including principals and supervisors, and approximately 34% on other administrative and support staff. In Japan, nearly 78% of school budgets is spent on teachers, none on principals and supervisors, and 22% on other administrative and support staff.

The report (National Commission on Teaching and America's Future, 1996) claims that most European and Asian countries

> do not spend more on education, but they invest more in teaching than in bureaucracy, hiring many fewer nonteaching staff and many more teachers who take on greater responsibility with greater supports. Like progressive firms, they work to get things right from the start. Rather than spend money on add-ons and band-aid programs to compensate for the failures of teaching they spend their education resources on what matters most: well-trained teachers who work intensively with students and with other teachers to improve teaching and learning. And they get better results. (p. 19)

This report is evidence and support that the Empowering Relationships (see Chapter 3) of the Humane Dimension could thrive better in a more leveled and circular organizational structure rather than a top-down structure (i.e., almost the opposite of Empowering Relationships).

The supports for classroom teachers in these European and Asian countries generally come in the form of professional development and time. A comparison of U.S. corporate expenditure for employee development with staff development for teachers shows that our schools provide paltry support. Estimates of professional development expenditures in schools range from only 1% to 3% of district operating budgets (National Commission on Teaching and America's Future, 1996, p. 40). In addition to limited financial support for professional development, U.S. teachers have "almost no regular time" to collaborate with each other about new teaching strategies. In many European and Asian countries, teachers are provided with substantial time to work with each other. For example, in Germany, Japan, and China, teachers:

- Spend 15 to 20 hours per week working with colleagues developing curriculum, counseling students, and engaging in independent study

- Routinely visit and observe other classrooms and other schools
- Attend seminars provided by other teachers and university faculty
- Conduct group study projects
- Participate in teacher-led study groups (p. 41)

In Japan and China, teachers conduct demonstration lessons for each other, discussing the flow of the lesson, potential student questions, and ways to build student interest. In Germany, teachers use time during the school day to develop instructional material and to examine student work in "curriculum conferences" (p. 41).

> ### Focus Group Response
>
> "I would like to see more professional reading taking place in study groups and discussion groups."

Here in the United States, classroom teachers typically are provided one or two district inservice days and, perhaps, two or three early release days for scheduled staff development. These learning opportunities are usually "brief encounters with packaged prescription offered by outside consultants" (Darling-Hammond, 1997, p. 320) who offer information "divorced from knowledge about how to interpret practice" (p. 319). The kind of professional development that works for teachers is based on a constructivist pedagogy and has these features:

> ### Focus Group Response
>
> "I'd love to spend more time watching colleagues teach. This really helps me see ideas put into practice."

- Connected to teachers' work with their students
- Linked to concrete tasks of teaching
- Organized around problem solving
- Informed by research
- Sustained over time by ongoing conversation and coaching (Darling-Hammond & McLaughlin, 1995, p. 598)

Perhaps the single most important feature of effective professional development is time. A district that is serious about providing teachers with genuine support for staff development will have to examine ways to provide the time teachers desperately need for their own growth. Some districts have begun adding meeting days to the beginning and the end of their school calendar. This approach can become substantially costly. Despite this cost, Sizer (1992) states, "Administrative budget targets should include substantial time for collective planning by teachers" (p. 208).

Raywid (1993) examined how schools across the country are making the time for teacher collaboration. Her investigation revealed that three broad approaches are used:

- Taking time now scheduled for other things
- Adding additional time to the school day and/or school year
- Altering staff utilization patterns—so that all administrators regularly do some teaching, for instance, or so that some teachers assume responsibility for more youngsters while other teachers meet. (p. 33)

Raywid (1993) highlighted the following specific examples of how these approaches for finding time are being used in schools:

- Teachers in an elementary school who are piloting new curriculum are scheduled for the same daily lunch period followed by a common preparation period for a total of 90 minutes of shared time each day.
- One high school is divided into various sections. One morning of every week, a section of students engages in community service, allowing their teachers to work together until the students return at noon.
- Some schools are able to finance extra teams of substitute teachers by increasing class size by just one or two students. Teams of teachers can meet frequently to plan units, deliberate on assessment, and so on when the substitutes cover their classes on a regular basis.
- Some districts have adopted a year-round calendar with quarterly three-week intersessions. Teachers use some of the break time for two- or three-day planning sessions.
- Some districts are rescheduling their mandatory three to five days per year of staff development and shifting to several two-hour sessions. Teachers are using this time for sustained, regularly scheduled collaboration.
- Some states are converting required instruction days (from 5 to 15) into staff development time.
- Many schools have discovered the benefits of regularly scheduled early dismissal of classes. This practice, when done two or three times a week, has been supplemented with time contributed by teachers so that three to four hours can be used for collaboration.
- Some schools extend the school day for 15 to 20 minutes, four days a week, and dismiss students at noon on the fifth day. Teachers use this half day for curriculum work and planning.
- Larger elementary schools schedule supplemental staff (e.g., art, music, physical education, computers, gifted, etc.) to meet with various classes in such a way as to provide regularly scheduled collaboration time for teams of teachers.
- One middle school scheduled a weekly Hobby Day, when all the adults in the building taught classes in their various interests. By carefully scheduling these exploratory units, teams of teachers were able to work together for a few hours every Friday. (pp. 31–32)

Watts and Castle (1993) provide further suggestions for finding time for teacher development (pp. 307–309). Flexibility in scheduling and staffing appears to be the primary consideration in their investigation of several schools who have found time for teachers. Five specific strategies for dealing with the dilemma of time include the following:

1. *Freed-up time.* Instead of restructuring the academic calendar, the school day, or teachers' schedules, this strategy uses different interventions to break teachers out of the traditional constraints such as the following:
   - Teaching assistants cover classes at regular intervals so that teachers can engage in collaborative planning.
   - Other teachers, principals, board office administrators, and support staff cover the classes of small groups of teachers on a regular basis.
   - Teachers involved in a curriculum innovation are provided two periods of released time during the project's pilot phase.
   - College interns and parent volunteers cover classes.
   - School-community collaborations, such as a high school and a community theatre, can lead to creative released time for teachers. Although students attend theatre productions, teachers are able to work on curriculum and planning.

2. *Restructured or rescheduled time.* Despite the complexities of changing traditional calendars, school days, and teaching schedules, some schools have found value in the permanent nature of this strategy by doing the following:
   - Schools are adding time to four days so that an early release occurs on the fifth day.
   - Some schools have created a first period before students arrive for teacher collaboration. The students stay longer in the afternoon, but the teachers are able to begin fresh without conflicting after-school duties interfering with the important work of teacher development.
   - High schools can use block scheduling to provide extended time for teacher collaboration during the day.

3. *Common time.* Schools that are serious about genuine transformation are moving beyond the traditional practice of isolated prep periods to experiment with common planning time involving teachers with similar responsibilities, such as the following:
   - Teachers involved in restructuring programs share two planning periods.
   - Teachers at the same grade level or on the same team or department have a common planning time.

4. *Better-used time.* Regularly scheduled faculty meetings in buildings are too often viewed as a waste of time. Many schools are using the

time set aside for meetings and staff development activities more efficiently:

- Teachers in many districts are expected to begin the school year by attending two or three days of central office meetings. In some districts, these central office meetings have been consolidated into a half or one whole day, leaving time for teacher preparation and planning.
- Monthly staff development newsletters are circulated in some schools to update faculty.
- School leadership teams, comprised of building administrators and teachers, handle administrative affairs so faculty meeting time can be spent on talking, thinking, and sharing.
- Information that is traditionally disseminated at faculty meetings can be posted daily on teacher bulletin boards or in memos or pass-and-read folders.
- In schools where each faculty member has a computer, e-mail can be used to circulate information in an expedient fashion.
- Single-issue faculty meetings facilitated by a faculty member can reduce the time wasted on general information sharing.

5. *Purchased time.* Within the current funding constraints, some schools are finding creative ways of purchasing time for teachers:
- "Substitute banks" of 30 to 40 days per year are set aside for teachers to use in full- or half-day increments for special professional development activities, committee work, and so on.
- Staff development funds can be used to pay stipends to teachers who are involved in staff development activities during the summer.
- Teacher partners who are carrying out a teaching innovation can share one teaching assignment between them.
- Limited foundation grants are available for schools involved in restructuring efforts. This money can be used to pay substitute teacher salaries.
- Some districts give "inservice credits" to teachers developing new programs on their own time. These credits can be used, in some places, for licensure and/or salary advancement.

These examples illustrate that the same flexibility and creativity that characterize constructivist classroom teaching approaches can be applied to staff development approaches as well. Raywid (1993) concludes her recommendations for finding time for teachers' professional growth with this call to action:

If collaborative endeavor is necessary to school adequacy, then *schools* must provide it. The responsibility rests with schools, not individual teachers. Further, administrators, policymakers, and public alike must accept a new conception of school time. If we are to redefine teachers' responsibilities to include collaborative sessions with colleagues—and both organizational research and teacher effectiveness research now suggests [*sic*] they are essential to good schools—then it is necessary to reconstrue teacher time. The time necessary to examine, reflect on, amend, and redesign programs is not *auxiliary* to teaching responsibilities—nor is it "released time" from them. It is absolutely central to such responsibilities, and essential to making schools succeed! (p. 34)

Given the *time*, the same guiding principles of a classroom constructivist pedagogy (Brooks & Brooks, 1993) have framed Roosevelt's staff development:

1. *Posing problems of emerging relevance to teachers* requires a deep understanding of issues teachers face in their classrooms and the connection of these issues to school restructuring.

2. *Structuring learning around primary concepts:* The quest for essence suggests an organization of information and knowledge around conceptual clusters, and not singular ideas or strategies. Teachers are professionals who are capable of working through the complexities and challenges of the "big ideas" of teaching. The "one-shot" workshop should be used less often.

3. *Seeking and valuing teachers' points of view* help make learning experiences both contextual and meaningful.

4. Assessing teacher learning in the context of individual professional *development* requires a shift in the traditional understanding of teacher evaluation. Rather than serving merely as a measurement of effectiveness, staff evaluations should be used to inform ongoing professional development. (pp. 35–98)

Summary

Professional growth, as this section has argued, cannot be mandated; nor can it be always fostered in an environment where traditional leadership is practiced, and trust is limited. Just as the goal of student learning in a constructivist setting is deep understanding, the goal of professional development is the same. The environment in which this kind of genuine learning can take place is the *Humane Dimension.* When **Communication is Based on Trust,** teachers are confident their emerging growth is following a meaningful and significant path. **Empowering Relationships** are present to share power with participants in their individual development. The **Purpose** of staff development is genuinely construed as **Other-Centered** in that student learning and colleague growth are paramount to individual teacher growth. Finally, both **Personal and Organizational Transformation** are the result of a constructivist pedagogy for professional development.

These conclusions about professional growth are what we have observed in our studies and especially at Roosevelt High School. Deeper understanding is observed constantly at this school, where teachers positively report on the professional autonomy to design their own learning.

ELEMENT 3: CURRICULUM-DRIVEN STAFF DEVELOPMENT

Bringing curriculum and instruction back together in the public school arena is one of several critical issues that goes to the heart of school reform. Not only have these two integral components of education been separated from each other, they have hardly been included, together or separately, in the nation's latest school reform movements. Over the past decade, as mentioned earlier, the literature on American school reform regales the reader about its "predictable failure" (Sarason, 1990) resulting from political mistreatment of the impoverished (Berliner & Biddle, 1995), bureaucratic structures (Astuto et al., 1994), limited notions of school leadership (Maxcy, 1991), and new state policies and changes in funding (Corcoran, Fuhrman, & Belcher, 2001). What is often overlooked in these dismal accounts of reform efforts is the very work of schools—curriculum and instruction. *What* we teach and *how* we teach, that is, the content and the procedures of schools, are too often omitted in the school reform debates. "How is it," asks Beane (1991), "that we can claim to speak of school reform without addressing the centerpiece of schools, the curriculum?" (p. 12). Also missing from the debate is a clear focus on instructional practices. General statements about how teachers should teach do not suffice when the result is student learning.

Curriculum and instruction have been omitted from the school reform debate and separated from each other in the Managerial Domain, where the focus is on explanations instead of deliberations (see Chapter 1). We are tripping over the elephant in the living room and calling each other clumsy! In our frustration and despair wrought by both internal and external finger pointing, we have turned to some common school practices to create a semblance of professional decorum. One of the practices is the tradition of staff development in our schools; another is the artificial barriers that are erected between various departments within school districts. Until these two practices are altered, the separation of curriculum and instruction from school reform efforts and from each other will continue to frustrate meaningful change in schools.

Traditional staff development in schools, characterized by "training," "faddism," "remote control," and "one-size-fits-all," is described in detail in the previous section. Despite all that we have learned about what works for students, that is, the lessons we have gleaned from years of experience, tomes of research, and constructivist practices, we revert to what too often does not work for teachers. The convenience of prepackaged training and the efficiency of top-down strategies have a stronghold on district thinking about staff development (Darling-Hammond & McLaughlin, 1995).

Even the ways we assess staff development effectiveness flies in the face of what we have learned about the authentic assessment of learning. According to Sparks and Hirsh (1997), the success of staff development "is judged by a 'happiness quotient' that measures participants' satisfaction with the experience and their off-the-cuff assessment regarding its usefulness" (p. 1). What these critics of traditional staff development call for is a radical rethinking characterized by critical reflection, teacher collaboration, new leadership roles for teachers, study groups, action research, and team planning.

> **Focus Group Response**
>
> "The courses and workshops are focused on the curriculum. Teacher needs are addressed."

Of course, this rethinking of staff development might not be so radical after all if the focus of critical reflection is not connected to student work. Teacher collaboration on *what* is the issue here. And unless these new leadership roles for teachers keep them in direct contact with students, the potential for meaningful change is school is limited. The other option for radical forms of professional development (i.e., study groups, action research, and team planning) must also be connected to what Schlechty (1997, 2001) calls "the business of schools"—designing meaningful and engaging work for students. To do otherwise is to risk a change without difference.

A second practice in schools that constrains meaningful reform and keeps us confined to the Managerial Domain is the way departments and grade levels (and, consequently, people and programs) operate in isolation from each other. Instead of a systems approach to reform, we focus on discrete and artificially detached "silos" within our organizations. Schlechty (2001) writes, "In a word, efforts to improve schools usually attend more to the introduction of projects and programs than to the systems in which these programs and projects are to be implemented" (p. 41). Rather than all areas within the organization supporting the work of change, we go about our business in separate meetings with separate plans and then wonder why we so often feel as if we are spinning our wheels. New academic standards for a content area come through from professional organizations and from state governments. The district staff in charge of curriculum goes about its business of developing curriculum. Meanwhile, budgets are projected with a dim awareness of textbook needs. District staff developers scan the horizon for future trends and popular workshop topics. Building administrators evaluate classroom teachers based on isolated teacher performances. New teachers participate in entry-year programs that may or may not be related to any of this other work. And more programs and committees are formed. In the meantime, veteran educators shake their heads, quietly close their classroom and office doors, and remain convinced that the real work of teachers is supervising the learning of students. All these other efforts seem like a waste of time because too often they occur outside the context of student learning. What could lend credibility and meaning to the work of curriculum developers, staff developers, teacher evaluators, and program facilitators is a concerted and connected focus on the work designed for students.

Focusing and coordinating curriculum and staff development initiatives require "major cultural changes" in schools (Corcoran et al., 2001). One way to coordinate and support our reform initiatives in schools is to change the way we do staff development and to tear down the barriers erected around our district. "What everyone appears to want for students—a wide array of learning opportunities that engage students in experiencing, creating, and solving real problems, using their own experiences, and working with others" (Lieberman, 1995, p. 591) should be the core of professional development in schools. Coordinated support could be accomplished slowly through what Darling-Hammond (1997) calls "an infrastructure for professional learning" (p. 598). The term "infrastructure" suggests focused, purposeful efforts. Imagine what could be done within the teacher culture if staff development became driven by curriculum development. Once that is done, professional appraisal designs could be tied to the goals of staff members as they go about enacting curriculum changes. Entry-year programs would be aligned with these same efforts. And on it could go with the one constant factor being a focus on the design of student work.

> **Focus Group Response**
>
> "This kind of staff development would be nonthreatening. Teachers could come up with ideas, and we would work in grade-level meetings with time to explore and talk."

Curriculum-Driven Staff Development Scenarios

A vision of curriculum-driven staff development has been shaped by a number of factors in recent years. One factor is the growing number of mandated entry-year programs for new teachers. A concerted effort to retain successful teachers has resulted in upgraded mentoring programs. These shifts have included advanced training in instructional analysis (e.g., Danielson, 1996, *Framework for Teaching*). In many districts, mentors are expected to work closely with their protégés within their classrooms and outside their classrooms. Another factor that has helped shape this vision of curriculum-driven staff development is the growth of standards-based education and the related academic content standards. The definition of standards-based education suggests the critical need for integrating curriculum and instruction in our staff development approaches. According to the Ohio Department of Education (2003), standards-based education is a process for planning, delivering, monitoring, and improving academic programs in which clearly defined academic content standards provide the basis for content in instruction and assessment. Standards provide the basis for the content that we teach. In other words, curriculum and instruction are finally united by what all students should know and be able to do, that is, standards. A third factor that has impacted curriculum-driven staff development is the gradual recognition of the need for more meaningful teacher leadership opportunities. The first section of this chapter, "Nontraditional Conceptions of Leadership," provided a detailed description of the need for and examples of expanded notions of teacher leadership. Teachers want to lead, not administrate. They deeply care about their students, and the leadership roles that they want to assume are those that are directly related to *what* their students learn and *how* they learn it. Curriculum-driven staff development is a natural arena for as yet unimagined teacher leadership roles and responsibilities.

Curriculum-Driven Staff Development
Scenario 1: Intermediate Reading

The fourth-, fifth-, and sixth-grade teachers in one school district returned to a new school year facing a real dilemma. Not only were they expected to teach new, and for several of these teachers, unknown, reading content standards, they were expected to do so with a reading series that had been purchased the year before. Most of the teachers agreed that they were barely familiar with the new reading series, and the thought of being held accountable for new standards was causing a great deal of stress.

By using the new reading curriculum as the focus of a yearlong staff development project, the district's reading coordinator was able to address the teachers' concerns about what to teach and how to teach it in a systematic, supportive way. For the first two months of school, the coordinator met with grade levels of teachers at each building during their lunchtimes. The primary objective of these sessions was to examine the new content standards. First, the teachers simply discussed what they thought each standard meant for their students. Then they shared what standards had been addressed in the previous year with the new reading series. Finally, the teachers were comfortable in identifying what standards they might not have addressed. Throughout the winter and spring, the reading coordinator met in three different half-day sessions with each group of grade-level teachers. These work sessions were aimed at creating new instructional materials that would help their students master the content standards. A lead teacher from each grade level designed and facilitated each session with the coordinator. The existing reading series was supplemented with new, teacher-made activities, units, and research packets. By the end of the school year, the materials were ready for printing. More importantly, the teachers were ready to apply the new learning from the sessions to other curriculum areas. For example, the teachers learned about technological innovations that could enhance student learning. They revisited Bloom's (1956) taxonomy to design activities at higher levels of thinking. They wrote, talked, and grew, just the way students in our classrooms do when engaging and meaningful work is given to them.

Curriculum-Driven Staff Development Scenario 2: English Department Course Alignment

During the past ten years, the English department at Roosevelt High School had changed. Several veteran teachers had retired, including the department chair. On assuming the chairperson position, Carol Danks realized that the combination of new faces and new curriculum could be viewed as an exciting opportunity for change or a recipe for disaster. Carol chose to view it as an opportunity and did so by using the new content standards as the driving force behind staff development.

> ### Focus Group Response
>
> "We need time. A 'pilot' period to work with the new curriculum before we are expected to try out new materials would be helpful."

The English department's work required time and collaboration. The main goal was to examine the content standards for direction and agreement about what would be taught in each course. In addition, the teachers who taught identical courses worked to create meaningful and similar assessments. To provide the time needed for this time of detailed, small-group work, the building principal helped set up a master schedule that allowed all the teachers in the department to have the same lunch period. The teachers agreed to meet a minimum of one period each week, often working three or four periods instead. The department chair helped by providing reference materials, technological support, and clerical assistance. Individual teachers gradually took on various leadership roles. For instance, one teacher became the department expert on rubric design. Another contributed in the area of ensuring academic integrity in student research. Leadership roles emerged as the teachers worked together on what and how they taught the students in their classrooms.

Curriculum-Driven Staff Development Scenario 3: Research Papers for the Young and the Old

A middle school language arts teacher was concerned that his students were leaving his eighth-grade classroom and entering the high school unprepared for writing research papers. He acknowledged that he addressed this area of the curriculum with lessons on research writing, but he knew the lessons were not as authentic as he would like them to be. When he expressed his concerns to the high school English teacher who taught a one-semester elective course called "Writing a Research Paper," the two of them embarked on a two-person curriculum-driven staff development project that resulted in meaningful work for both the eighth graders and the seniors.

> ### Focus Group Response
>
> "We would have opportunities to ask each other questions."
>
> "Teachers would get to observe each other in their classrooms."

First, the two teachers examined the content standards for both grade areas and identified how the two sets were related. Along with other, more advanced standards, the seniors and the eighth graders were expected to know and be able to do similar things! The two teachers agreed to meet two goals within the last month of the semester. After writing three increasingly more sophisticated research papers, the seniors had to design a series of lessons on legitimate paraphrasing and locating sources of information in the library and on the Internet. Then the seniors came to the middle school during their Research class period for seven days. Each senior worked with two eighth graders in a series on their individually designed lessons on exploratory reading, citing sources, using transitions in writing, and making a reference page.

In order for the seniors and the eighth graders to experience this authentic learning opportunity, the two language arts teachers had to use their curriculum to design a unit of instruction that spanned two buildings. These teachers agree that they learned just as much, if not more, than their students, because they worked together on a task that was important to them.

ELEMENT 4: APPRAISAL SYSTEMS FIT FOR A CULTURE OF PROFESSIONAL WORTH

We have argued earlier in this chapter that a constructivist pedagogy for student learning can be and should be applied to teacher learning. Now we take a look at the appraisal systems that are used to evaluate teachers by comparing best practice in assessment of student learning to typical practices in professional evaluations. Current practitioners advocate for the authentic assessment of student learning. Yet how authentic are the professional assessments of teachers? How many districts continue to use a checklist of "effective teacher" behaviors to evaluate faculty members? Why can't the appraisal systems that we use with our teachers be authentic, alternative, and/or performance-based? We must ask ourselves what we value when we go about evaluating. If we value adherence to fixed, prescriptive routines in the classroom, then certainly, checking off items such as "States lesson objectives at the beginning of the lesson" and "Uses more than one modality in the lesson" will suffice. If, however, we value reflective practice and teacher collaboration, the traditional appraisal designs will no longer promote professional growth.

The traditional appraisal systems are designed to do one thing well— they expose incompetent teachers. Fullan and Hargreaves (1996) ask, "How many teachers do you think are irretrievably incompetent? It is likely no higher than 2% or 3%" (p. 10). So a high school faculty of 100 teachers routinely jumps through the hoops of an evaluation system that is based on a clinical supervision model created for student teachers (i.e., preconference, observation, postconference). The two or three incompetent teachers are discovered, and, if there is time, they receive a sufficient amount of guidance and support from a building principal or staff development supervisor. What do we do about the other 98 teachers? More than likely their unique forms of effectiveness and competence remain undetected by the appraisal format, and they, in turn, develop in spite of the evaluation. Fullan and Hargreaves go on:

> Many teachers are very effective. Their problem is lack of access to other teachers. Access would mean that they could become even better while sharing their expertise. Many other teachers are competent but could improve considerably if they were in a more collaborative environment. If such an environment existed from the very beginning of their careers they would be dramatically better. Those teachers who are ineffective have either become so through years of unproductive and alienating experiences, or were ill-suited for teaching from the beginning. Imposing punitive appraisal schemes for all is like using a sledgehammer to crack a nut. It reduces "appraisal" to the lowest common denominator. Appraisal schemes that implicate 100% of the staff to detect a small percentage of incompetents are a gross waste of time. Ironically, the anxiety they generate can also hold back the excellence of the many as they become reluctant to take risks for fear of punishment. (p. 10)

Traditional Teacher Appraisal Schemes

Current teacher evaluation systems are too often nonproductive and burdensome to both the teacher and the principal. The time and effort put into this exercise in accountability typically do not result in anyone's growth. In their work on teacher evaluations that enhance professional practice, Danielson and McGreal (2000) identify the following six main areas of deficiency that have led to our flawed appraisal systems:

1. *Outdated, limited, evaluative criteria.* Current appraisal schemes rely on the documentation of observable behaviors that are thought to increase student learning. The research that informed these beliefs relied on limited measures of student achievement: "norm-referenced, machine-scorable, multiple-choice tests of fairly low-level knowledge" (p. 3). Over the past three decades our goals for student achievement have evolved to include more complex learning and higher levels of thinking. Traditional teacher appraisal schemes assessed the best of what could be known at the time. Our profession has developed over the years from ongoing research. Pedagogical practices have kept pace; so must appraisal practices. Danielson and McGreal (2000) contend that

> the evaluative criteria used should represent the most current research available; and we need to make provisions, as time goes on, to revise those criteria to reflect current finds. For example, teachers might be asked to demonstrate that their students are successfully achieving the state's content standards, or that they are teaching for understanding (rather than merely rote learning). (p. 4)

2. *Few shared values and assumptions about good teaching.* The gradual shift from a behaviorist emphasis in the classroom to a constructivist emphasis has caused most educators to develop their own personal opinions about what good teaching is. These beliefs go unshared in districts with appraisal systems that prevent teachers and administrators from discussing opinions about best practice. "As a result, teachers can only guess at the values and assumptions about good teaching on which their performance will be judged" (Danielson & McGreal, 2000, p. 4).

3. *Lack of precision in evaluating performance.* The ratings on most appraisal schemes lack validity and even meaning to most teachers for several reasons. The first reason is that there is little agreement on rating scales such as "needs improvement" or "satisfactory." We do not have the equivalent benchmarks such as those found on rubrics for evaluating student work. The second reason is that the full use of the rating scale is seldom used. In most schools, teachers, particularly veteran teachers, expect to receive all "outstanding" ratings regardless of the quality of their teaching or their definition of outstanding. Another reason that most appraisal systems are not deemed valid is that some administrators are "reluctant to be completely honest in their evaluations of teaching" (p. 4). This reluctance has to do with a practice that is known as "the dance of the lemons." Here is what we mean. A principal sees that a teacher is not performing well and would like to see the teacher removed from the faculty. However, to avoid a dismissal, the principal recommends a transfer to another building. A transfer would be difficult if the teacher has received poor evaluations. Hence, "the dance of the lemons" and seriously compromised appraisals exist.

4. *Hierarchical, one-way communication.* Traditional teacher evaluations consist of a one-shot gathering of data based on a single classroom observation. Regardless of the climate surrounding evaluations, "the teacher's role is essentially passive" (Danielson & McGreal, 2000, p. 5). Teachers just wait to hear the results about their effectiveness as teachers on the basis of a 50-minute observation.

5. *No differentiation between novice and experienced practitioners.* Without a period of apprenticeship enjoyed by most other professions, new teachers are expected to teach at the same level as experienced teachers. Novices in the classroom are typically held to the same standard as veterans. The same checklist of teacher behaviors is held up in both classrooms.

6. *Limited administrator expertise.* Although good teaching can be recognized in many different settings, teaching is highly contextual. For example, knowledge of content and developmental levels of learning among different students is quite relevant to teaching. As Danielson and McGreal (2000) put it, "Many teachers are more expert regarding their work than the administrators who 'supervise' them—more knowledgeable about their discipline, current pedagogical approaches, or the developmental characteristics of the students they teach" (p. 6). The result is that teachers are not confident in sharing specific concerns about their classroom instruction with a principal whose expertise may be limited. The assessment process becomes a practice characterized by routine and superficiality.

Teacher Appraisal in the Managerial Domain

In the Managerial Domain, the focus is on maintaining the existing system. It is little wonder that traditional teacher appraisal schemes have remained entrenched in our schools. These appraisal schemes help ensure that the teacher culture and the administrator culture remain apart by diminishing the role of principal to manager rather than true instructional leader. Danielson and McGreal (2000) find most teacher evaluation systems to be characterized by "top-down communication, in which the only evidence of teacher performance is that collected by an administrator during classroom observations" (p. 5). Furthermore, this communication is more about explanation than dialogue. The primary purpose of these traditional appraisal schemes is to protect the existence of the system more than it is to promote the professional development of the teacher. Unfortunately, in most districts, teachers and administrators agree in contractual form to perpetuate this form of professional evaluation. Both groups have a vested interest in keeping the appraisal system intact. Teachers may not want to give up what little control or freedom they have within the privacy of their classrooms. Going through a traditional appraisal is much safer than exposing one's real concerns about classroom practices. Principals seldom have enough time as it is to conduct the checklist approach to teacher evaluations. Appraisals that aim for teacher reflection and faculty collaboration will take more time. Furthermore, the predictable, linear nature of traditional appraisals takes the guesswork out of growth. In the postconference with the administrator, the teacher can agree to do what it takes to get to the next level of competency, and then can go back to teaching.

Teacher Appraisal in the Humane Dimension

Before we consider how teacher appraisals could look within the Humane Dimension, it is important to emphasize that organizational transformation is the ultimate outcome of personal transformation. In the Managerial Domain, an individual's growth is typically confined to that one person. A teacher may begin using alternative forms of assessment in his or her classroom, but because of teacher isolation and professional evaluations that do not address this aspect of teacher decision making, his or her ideas may spread only to a friend or two. In the Humane Dimension, relationship building increases the potential for growth,

> **Focus Group Response**
>
> "My teaching skills wouldn't be evaluated based on a single observation; the process would take place over time."

both on an individual level and, ultimately, on an organizational level. The cycle of relationship building begins with a single face-to-face encounter and gradually expands outward to include many others. This process occurs when the four components of relationship building are enacted, that is, Communication Based on Trust, Empowering Relationships, Other-Centered Purpose, and Personal and Organizational Transformation.

It is our contention that in the Humane Dimension, appraisals of most teachers in a district would be characterized by ongoing peer collaborations through the process of action research. (Entry-year teachers, because of licensing standards and mandates, should be required to go through a form of clinical supervision, mentoring, and observations, whereas tenured teachers needing assistance may benefit from the focused support described previously.) Danielson and McGreal (2000) offer a thorough description of a three-track evaluation system in their book, *Teacher Evaluation: To Enhance Professional Practice*. Their second track, "The Professional Development Track," is designed to help the majority of teachers "achieve higher professional competence and expand their understanding of self, role, context, and career" (p. 99).

Action research is the basic framework of our proposed teacher appraisal scheme. According to Mills (2003), action research is any systematic inquiry conducted by teacher researchers to gather information about how they teach and how well their students learn. The information

Focus Group Response

"Peer evaluations and peer coaching would take place."

is "gathered with the goals of gaining insight, developing reflective practice, effecting positive changes in the school environment (and on educational practices in general), and improving student outcomes and the lives of those involved" (p. 5). Mills states,

> Action research is research done *by* teachers *for* themselves; it is not imposed on them by someone else. Action research engages teachers in a four-step process:
>
> 1. Identify an area of focus
> 2. Collect data
> 3. Analyze and interpret data
> 4. Develop an action plan (p. 5)

When teachers work together in this process, collaborative action research results. Sagor (1997) contends that

> one would have to look long and hard to find a single school endeavor that incorporates more of the essential findings of the change literature than collaborative action. This type of professional work builds on *felt needs*; participation in it is *voluntary*; it focuses on *educationally critical issues*; the strategy calls for *mutual adaptation*; the resultant data build *teacher efficacy*; when properly implemented, the participants receive *ample support*; and what participants learn from information, as it is uncovered, *puts pressure on them* to change. (pp. 169–170)

Glickman (1995) sees action research as a way to bring teachers and administrators together for one common purpose. "The reason everyone goes into education," he states in his video, "is to have a powerful influence on the educational lives of students. Action research helps reinforce and cement the belief that together [teachers and administrators] can make a difference." Check (1997) writes that this type of teacher inquiry "can be a revolutionary form of professional development because it responds in a new way to a fundamental question: who can validly generate knowledge about teaching and learning?" (p. 7). Powerful professional development can result from action research by "offering the possibility of major, long-term changes that are generated by teachers themselves, based on their own investigations of practice" (p. 7).

Our proposed teacher appraisal scheme, which is based on action research, is characterized more by compassion than managerial systems; that is, it rightfully belongs in the Humane Dimension. Thus, our "Appraisal System Fit for a Climate of Professional Worth" is undergirded by the four components of the Humane Dimension.

> **Focus Group Response**
>
> "Individuals choose the areas they want to work on in the evaluation process."

Teacher Appraisal and Communication Based on Trust

As explained in the second chapter, trust is the beginning of the cycle of human connectedness. Trust means "to rely on someone," "to have faith in someone," "to confide in someone," and "to expect confidently from someone." In the Humane Dimension, a teacher's professional appraisal would begin with Trust. After identifying a teaching area in need of refinement, a problem area, or a concern, the teacher would choose from a list of teacher leaders that individual who has the expertise and skills best aligned with the targeted area. This teacher leader would serve as a research advisor to the teacher whose growth would be determined by the progress made in the action research process and the conclusions reached. The cyclic nature of action research means that as one conclusion is reached, another question is formed.

Teacher Appraisal and Empowering Relationships

In Chapter 3, we included Kreisberg's (1992) definition of empowerment as "the ability to make a difference, to participate in decision making, and to take action for change. Empowerment does not assume control of resisting others, but emerges from work with others who are also deciding, acting, and making a difference" (p. xi). Freeman (1998) sees that action research empowers individual teachers because, "In moving from interests and questions that are completely embedded in local circumstances and experience to a larger disciplinary framework of teaching, teacher-research is defining its own territory. Teachers are creating, in their own terms, a new and viable community around the ideas and issues of teaching that are central to their work" (p. 13). As individuals begin to see the differences that they can make by sharing a focus on teaching issues, small groups of teachers begin to grow and change until, eventually, a critical mass of faculty members is transformed.

Teacher Appraisal and Other–Centered Purpose

The primary focus of a teacher leader who is supporting a teacher researcher is that other person's growth. Assistance is emphasized more than assessment in this model: listening, understanding, and accepting evidence of continuous support. The servant-leader model comes to life when action research becomes the primary mode of teacher appraisal.

Teacher Appraisal and Personal and Organizational Transformation

Action research requires teachers to draw on current research and to add to their current knowledge. Done in collaboration with other teachers, action research "changes the context and provides a way of organizing collective work so that professional expertise is tended and extended, helping to build a strong professional learning community" (Calhoun, 2002, p. 23). Action research is, by its very nature, a public act of sharing (Freeman, 1998). My growth influences your growth. Together, our growth extends throughout our grade level, our team, or our department until eventually, an entire school witnesses the changes going on in our professional lives.

Summary

In the Kent City School District and at Roosevelt High School, teachers are given a choice of two evaluation models: a traditional checklist of items to be examined during a 30- to 60-minute observation conducted up to four times in a school year or an alternative assessment containing a reflective practice cycle of unit planning and mutual goal setting by the teacher and administrator. Over the years, the alternative assessment has continued to grow as the first choice of teachers.

APPLYING THE HUMANE DIMENSION

Specific staff development activities for incorporating the elements of a transformed teacher culture are essentially the same as those activities listed in Resources A, B, C, and D. That is, activities for developing the Humane Dimension's components are the main focus of our work, which eventually leads to transformed organizational cultures. However, we do recognize the need to recommend some specific activities from our notebooks of Professional Development Notepad exercises that specifically relate to the four elements of both the Transformed Leadership Culture and the Transformed Teacher Culture. The following exercises are offered as only a beginning to understanding the infrastructure of these two cultures.

ELEMENT 1 EXERCISE

Nontraditional Conceptions of Leadership

Leadership roles for teachers can be firmly rooted within a school's culture when run-of-the-mill materials such as books for study groups, office supplies, and meeting refreshments are routinely provided to leaders. Like all leaders, teacher leaders benefit from exposure to new ideas and innovative practices.

- Actively seek out with teacher leaders people within and outside the district who share common interests.
- Help arrange visits to other schools and schedule collaborative planning time for stronger, more purposeful leadership.
- Set aside time for reading journal articles and books. Reading professional literature is too often a luxury for busy educators. Perhaps the same kind of regularly scheduled sustained silent reading opportunities provided to elementary students (e.g., *Drop Everything And Read*) could be offered to our faculty members as well.
- Make professional reading material available to faculty members, too, through a cooperative effort of individual teachers and administrators sharing what they are reading. Faculty members who subscribe to professional journals could share the table of contents of monthly journals and ask others to decide which articles they would enjoy reading. Book talks could become regular faculty meeting agenda items.

ELEMENT 2 EXERCISE

Constructive Practices for Teachers Exercise

The shotgun approach to much staff development discourages deep thinking about pedagogical issues. Sustaining staff development over time requires a group effort. Administrators and teachers should share in the planning of leadership roles so that professional growth is treated in an ongoing, developmental manner. Lead roles that typically sustain staff development practices include trainers, peer coaches, study group leaders, and program evaluators. Many schools are using innovative ways to find time for professional development activities. We find that student exhibitions and community service are two student-centered learning practices that, if structured effectively, can result in nonclassroom instructional experiences for teachers.

- Through the careful use of adult volunteers, teachers can be provided regularly scheduled time for opportunities such as study groups and collaborative assessment design.

- Interschool collaborations can energize teaches who are interested in exploring common professional issues. For example, there is immeasurable value in collaborative study among elementary and high school teachers. What can emerge is a heightened awareness that masterful teaching transcends subject matter and learner age.
- Professional journaling is another way to move from imitative behavior to deeper understanding. Teachers can be encouraged to record journal entries about new practices. Reflecting on their behaviors and insights can be a powerful professional development strategy.

ELEMENT 3 EXERCISE

Curriculum-Driven Staff Development Exercises

1. *Common Planning Time Exercise.* Classroom teachers need time to immerse themselves in content standards and curriculum. Through careful design of a building's master schedule, grade levels and departments can be given common planning time. For instance, during those years when a new science course of study is being initiated, middle school and high school science teachers can share the same prep period. At the elementary level, some (or all, if possible) teachers in the same grade level can also have built into their schedules that same non-classroom-teaching time. Once or twice a week, this time may be used for curriculum review, assessment design, and so on.

2. *Grade-Level Collaboration Exercise.* Designing units of instruction in collaboration with grade-level peers has many advantages. Teachers review and gain a deeper understanding of the content standards and grade-level indicators through discussion. Common assessments can be established and a wide variety of learning activities can be created. Later, teachers share discussion results between grade levels.

3. *Assessment Collaboration Exercise.* The design of short-cycle assessment of student learning is a critical need in schools as standards-based education grows in prominence across the country. Using the staff development hours and days set aside by most districts for this curricular area could result in valuable professional development. Teachers could spend time studying professional literature on these assessments. They could also view a professionally developed videotape series on the topic. Assessment samples

could be examined. At the core of all this staff development activity could be student learning.

4. *Cross-Grade Collaboration Exercise.* Another way to deepen the understanding of curriculum is thoughtful cross-grade examination of what students should know and be able to do. Upper elementary-grade teachers want and need to know what their students are learning in the primary grades. Middle school teachers want and need to know what was going on before the students came to their school as well as what is expected at the high school. High school teachers are part of the curriculum chain as well. Again, time should be set aside for this cross-grade sharing of curriculum. Discussions should focus on the spiral effect of single concepts from Grades K–12.

ELEMENT 4 EXERCISE

Appraisal Systems Fit for a Culture of Professional Worth

1. *Common Goal Study Groups.* A basic premise of constructivism is that learning is optimized through varying degrees of social inter-action. An assessment approach that can strengthen the "value" in "evaluation" would involve small groups of educators who are targeting similar professional goals. Every school year, a small percentage of faculty members are up for professional evaluation. By establishing growth targets early in the year, groups could be formed around common goals. For example, one administrator and three classroom teachers may be particularly concerned about how much students are engaged in their classroom work. This group could establish both individual goals and common group goals for a year's work collaboratively on a review of professional literature on the topic. As the year progresses, the group would meet twice a month to discuss what they are reading and what they are observing in their individual practices. Peer observations could also be a part of this collaboration.

2. *Portfolios Connected to Mission Statement.* When a school's mission statement is the foundation of teachers' work, the mission's potential for success is vastly increased. A critical part of individual evaluations should be their grasp of and work toward the mission statement. Assessing this aspect of professional growth could

be accomplished through a portfolio comprised of items such as interview notes, journal entries, and activity logs.

3. *Peer Teaching and "Brown Bag" Sessions.* One strategy that can indicate mastery of a topic or practice is the successful teaching of that topic or practice. Part of a professional evaluation could include evidence of peer teaching. A classroom teacher who has worked on anecdotal record keeping in assessing student learning probably has spent considerable time developing this skill. He or she has studied the theory behind alternative assessments. He or she has examined various record-keeping strategies and tools, and he or she has experimented, through trial and error, with different ways to record observations of students in the classroom. Other teachers would benefit greatly from this work. Part of this teacher's evaluation, then, could include a detailed description of his or her teaching about anecdotal record keeping in the building or district. Perhaps lunchtime "brown bag" sessions could be held four times during the evaluation year. A newsletter or videotape may be other ways to share his or her expertise.

4. *School-Community Collaboration.* An area of professional growth that is often missing from evaluation designs has to do with school-community collaborations. Students benefit when educators work with agencies, businesses, and organizations within the school's community. For instance, part of a guidance counselor's evaluation might include his or her work with local support groups such as mental health agencies and children services. Classroom teachers could be encouraged to develop links with local businesses or social service clubs.

REFLECTION

When you proceed through Chapter 9 on Evidence of the Humane Dimension in Schools, reflect after reading each educator's comments on how you might incorporate your new knowledge into staff development opportunities and into your own life.

8

Handling Challenges and Pitfalls

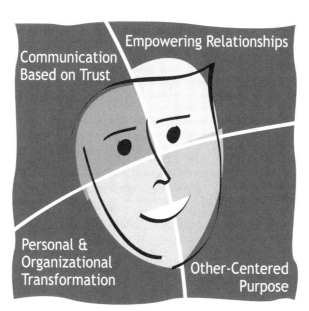

Humane Dimension

The first seven chapters of this book have spelled out, in painstaking detail, what is meant by the Humane Dimension. Chapter 1 offered a definition of the Humane Dimension and discussed its need in organizations such as schools. The next four chapters focused on each of the four components of the Humane Dimension—Communication Based on Trust, Empowering Relationships, Other-Centered Purpose, and Personal and Organizational Transformation. The primary purpose of these five chapters and the two chapters on elements of transformed leadership and teacher cultures was to share with the reader our conviction that there must be a better way for people to live with each other and to work together in schools.

Few people who have worked in public education would disagree that *how* we are currently interacting with each other is constraining school transformation. As stated in Chapters 2 through 5, evidence to that end abounds. Administrative teams read book after book on successful leadership, borrowing the ideas and imitating the behaviors of business executives and retired politicians. We genuinely want to do better and keep hoping that Project A or Approach B or Guiding Coalition C will be the one best answer. But seldom do we do the following two things:

1. Agree on what the challenges or problems are

2. Face the inevitable issue of pitfalls and failure

So we stay in the Managerial Domain and call it home. We decorate the walls with motivational posters and rearrange the furniture according to the latest decision-making fad. We expend untold energy doing something, anything, to make our schools better. Rarely do we talk in open, adult fashion about what the real problems are. Even more rarely do we know how to deal with the inevitable failure of our work (Sarason, 1990).

We cite an example used by Kegan (2000) of a faculty leadership council meeting from the perspective of Lynn, the chair of a junior high school English department. One of Lynn's colleagues, the history chair, proposed a one-year experiment on faculty evaluations. The proposal was an attempt to move beyond the traditional teacher evaluation conducted by the principal, who observed teachers twice in a school year. Kegan's description of the time-worn tradition says so much:

> They announced visits, so teachers end up preparing for a performance, which they resent and which is a lousy basis for evaluation. The teachers don't feel that the principal gets a fair sample of their work. The kids know what's going on and act weird—they're on "good behavior" too, and completely unspontaneous. The principal writes up a generally innocuous report, which the teacher then pours [sic] over like an old Kremlinologist trying to detect the hidden

meaning in some routine public communique. Usually there is no hidden meaning. The principal is just discharging a duty that she finds as unpleasant and unrewarding as the teachers. Nobody is learning a thing but at least the principal can tell the central office that "everyone's been evaluated" and she has the paperwork, neatly typed in the files, to prove it. (p. 37)

The proposal presented for the leadership council to consider would be based on peer collaboration and individual teacher action research. This peer evaluation process would be tried out for a year with an ongoing assessment of how it was promoting teacher development. Kegan (2000) shares Lynn's frustrations with how the proposal was stalled in the leadership council where, after three long discussions, the real merits of the proposal were ignored, and the implicit problems the proposal was trying to address were never acknowledged.

Why do we do this? Why do we convince ourselves that we are engaging in meaningful, important discussions when, in fact, we are skirting around the issues? We can just imagine those three long discussions about peer evaluations through which Lynn sat on the leadership council. The principal expected that "it couldn't be done" because of contractual agreements and past practices. In extending Kegan's (2000) fictional school dilemma, we imagine the following scenario.

Four teachers nodded in agreement with the principal and described their own commitment to "teach the way they always do no matter who came into the room." Only Lynn and two other council members, including the department chair who proposed the idea in the first place, expressed an interest in the idea of peer evaluations. They described their own frustrations with the limited number of observations and the "phony feel" of the process. They described some articles they had read about teachers involved in peer evaluations in other districts. What stood out for Lynn and the other two council members was that peer evaluations could lead to meaningful and substantial teacher growth. Finally, at the fourth meeting, Lynn shared copies of the articles referenced in an earlier meeting. Council members agreed to read the material. When they reconvened, it was the middle of the second semester. A central office administrator was invited to join the council's discussion. After two more meetings and at least two private conversations between the principal and the central office administrator, the proposed peer evaluation was approved for piloting in a modified form. Four members of the social studies department who volunteered to engage in peer evaluations were given the green light to try it out for one year. These four teachers were expected to report their findings, concerns, and recommendations in quarterly presentations to the leadership council.

How many readers believe that at the end of the pilot, peer evaluations will replace traditional evaluations in Lynn's school?

We expect that the proposed reform of professional evaluation will, at best, be watered down to a peer coaching or mentoring program. At worst, it will die a quick death by the end of the school year. We believe this for two reasons. First, challenges and problems were not acknowledged, and, second, the proposal's inevitable pitfalls and failures were not addressed. Thus another example of professionals not talking openly, not facing the real problem, and avoiding the inevitable possibility of failure has prevented school transformation from coming to fruition.

WHAT ARE THE CHALLENGES AND PROBLEMS?

At the center of the most frustrating encounters educators experience in schools (or, we argue, spouses encounter in marriages, associates encounter in businesses, congregations encounter in churches, etc.) is our incredible inability to acknowledge the implicit problems embedded in the school culture. At an even deeper, more tacit level, each person is too often unwilling to share his or her own concerns about reform proposals.

The first necessity in determining the real problem is the willingness to acknowledge that implicit problems do exist. Our tendency to treat discourse as debate causes us to view the purpose of group discussion to win an argument "rather than to understand different ways of thinking . . . and to get things done" (Mezirow, 2000, p. 12). When we reduce a discussion about an alternative approach to teacher evaluation to a debate about the pros and cons of traditional evaluations, we miss many opportunities to uncover the hidden problems. So, like Lynn's colleagues, we spend time discussing the legalities of peer evaluations, for example. We defend, and we argue. We rush to take a stand on how right or how wrong peer evaluations are as if this topic can be reduced to a debate. What should be discussed instead are the challenges and problems that peer evaluations could resolve, such as the following:

- The principal does not have sufficient time to evaluate all teachers in a meaningful way.
- Teachers need time to identify growth goals and to develop growth plans.
- Some teachers may be reluctant to share their self-assessed areas of weaknesses with their principal.
- Schools are not collaborative settings; instead, they tend to promote isolation and, to a degree, competition.
- Teachers should know much about classroom instruction and should be expected to support each other in a peer evaluation context.

The leadership council could have and should have used their meeting times to discuss these issues. Such discussions may lead to the identification of other problems associated with traditional teacher evaluations. More importantly, such discussions could lead to critical reflection about teacher evaluations until, eventually, multiple solutions could be identified. It may well end up that peer evaluation is only one of many approaches to teacher evaluations that are *of value* to all faculty members.

The second necessity in determining the real problem is that each person must be willing to share his or her own concerns about reform proposals. Instead of hiding concerns and distancing from blame, the participants in the deliberation should be forthright with their legitimate and not so legitimate concerns. Principals may feel that they are to blame for apparent weaknesses of the traditional teacher evaluations. Experienced teachers may want to keep the evaluations the way they have always been for fear of being exposed as weak instructors. The number of individual concerns with a proposed change is more than likely equal to or greater than the number of people in the discussion. This is because schools are places where adults

- Are uncomfortable with ambiguity
- Avoid negative talk
- Defer to authority
- Need order and predictability
- Protect themselves behind titles
- Fear negative consequences

Until we come to share our concerns honestly and openly, schools will continue to be, as Pinnel and Wayson (in draft form) put it, "childish organizations" attempting to reform "failure-oriented systems."

DEALING WITH PITFALLS AND FAILURE: A CONVERSATION WITH THE REVEREND BRUCE CHOUINARD

Dr. Bruce Chouinard is the pastor of Grace Baptist Church in Kent, Ohio. Extended conversations and a long lunch with us in the fall of 2003 have led to the following section, inspired by Bruce, a scholar and our close friend.

Observations that public schools are "failure-oriented systems" (Pinnell & Wayson, in draft form) or are doomed to inevitable failure (Sarason, 1990) are harsh criticisms; we do not share this extreme position with these authors. But unless we are willing to face the inevitable issue of failure, we will remain in the Managerial Domain. This same position can be shared with regard to any human grouping or institution. Families. Businesses. Church congregations. Why? *Because we are human.* We make mistakes about our own strengths. We are tempted to think we are bigger and better than we may be. We are sometimes blind to our own need for approval and power. And we often refuse to let go of projects or programs long after their purposes have been served.

Our unwillingness and our inability to deal with the inevitable failures of life lead us to act in certain, almost predictable ways. We engage in self-justification and self-protections when instead we could practice extreme humility.

Imagine a situation in a middle school where a team leader named Julie teaches seventh-grade social studies and math. Julie has fifteen years' experience teaching middle school and has championed a number of recent innovations in her school including assessment literacy and curriculum mapping. Her role as a teacher leader stood out among her peers as one who promoted collaboration and fostered meaningful growth. In the past few years, however, Julie has seemed more intent on building her own reputation as an outstanding teacher and less focused on helping the students in her classroom. Evidence to this end includes incomplete interim reports and several lost student projects. Students and parents have begun to express their concerns.

When Rick, the building assistant principal, discusses the situation with Julie, he begins by expressing his appreciation and acknowledgment of her abilities as both a teacher and an instructional leader. He goes on to share his concerns by describing specific incidents that highlight Julie's negligence of her students.

Julie's reaction is to justify her behaviors by enumerating all her responsibilities as a team leader. The conversation within the assistant principal's office is more argument than discussion. Julie's self-justification leads to self-protection. As her wall of defenses goes up, so does Rick's. His remarks about the need to refocus on student learning sound incriminating to Julie. Her comments about the need for somebody to provide staff development to the teachers in the building are equally incriminating to Rick. And so it goes. Rick feels an equal need to justify and protect his work as an administrator.

In stark contrast to the reactions in this example is the Humane Dimension's third component, Other-Centered Purpose. The core of this component is humility, which is the other side of self-justification and self-protection. Had Julie been able to engage in a discussion (instead of an argument), she might have admitted, first to herself and then to Rick, that growing as a teacher leader had become exciting and rewarding. Likewise, if Rick had been able to acknowledge how he had grown to depend on Julie's skills in facilitating staff development throughout the building, he may have entered the conversation differently.

The move from self-justification to humility requires forgiveness. To let go of the need to protect our images means we will have to have faith in something other than ourselves. This will give us the freedom to say,

"Sometimes I am not as talented, as wise, as trustworthy, as I should be."
Yet how can we speak of words such as *humility, forgiveness, faith,* and *freedom* in a secular setting such as public schools? We respond by asking,
"How can't we?" If we no longer want to be characterized by the ordinary,
then we will have to begin working these words into our vocabulary. If
we want to move from the Managerial Domain to the Humane Dimension,
we will simply have to cease being small and ordinary and become the
profoundly compassionate people we were meant to be. After all, as Parker
Palmer (1998) explains so clearly in his work *The Courage to Teach,* education
reform cannot happen as long as educators continue to live "divided lives":

> Many of us know from personal experience how it feels to live a
> divided life. Inwardly, we experience one imperative for our lives,
> but outwardly we respond to quite another. This is the human con-
> dition, of course—our inner and outer worlds are never in perfect
> harmony. But there are extremes of dividedness that become intol-
> erable, when one can no longer live without bringing one's actions
> into harmony with one's inner life. When that happens inside of
> one person, then another, and another, and another, in relation to a
> significant social issue, a movement may be conceived. . . .
>
> The condition to be overcome by living divided no more has a
> specific etiology. We inhabit institutional settings, including school
> and work and civic society, because they harbor opportunities that
> we value. But the claims those institutions make on us are some-
> times at odds with out hearts—for example, the demand for loyalty
> to the corporation, right or wrong, versus the inward imperative to
> speak truth. That tension can be creative, up to a point. It becomes
> pathological when the heart becomes a wholly owned subsidiary
> of the organization, when we internalize organizational logic and
> allow it to overwhelm the logic of our lives.
>
> To live divided no more is to find a new center for one's life,
> a center external to the institution and its demands. This does not
> mean leaving the institution physically; one may stay at one's post.
> But it does mean taking one's spiritual leave. (p. 167)

FOUR LEVELS IN DEALING WITH FAILURE

Taking a spiritual leave means that one finds "solid ground on which to
stand outside the organization—the ground of one's own being—and from
that ground is better able to resist the deformations that occur when organizational values become the landscape of one's inner life" (Palmer, 1998,
pp. 168–169). In other words, we may have to step outside of our school
selves and use words that are not part of our teacher talk and, perhaps, we
may just need to use our "outside voices" when we come face-to-face with

the inevitable failure of our work. Chouinard (personal communication, July 11, 2003) sees four levels in dealing with failure in individuals and within organizations:

Level 1. Understand the principle

Level 2. Know when the principle applies

Level 3. Have the power to change

Level 4. Deal with the failure

The strength to face failure starts within the individual and progresses outward to the next individual until, in time, a critical mass of people "live divided no more" (Palmer, 1998, p. 167).

Failing in Our Communications Based on Trust

Each time we met with a focus group of teachers and administrators who reviewed our progress on this book, someone said this exact sentence, "It all begins with **Trust**." What they meant by this was that in order for school reform to result in transformation, people within the school must trust each other. Chouinard (personal communication, July 11, 2003) sees the four levels of dealing with failure in our communications that *should be* based on trust in the following way:

Level 1. All faculty members must be on board that trust is a good foundation for its communications.

Level 2. Faculty members will have to know when the principle applies and under which circumstances they may be tempted not to be trustworthy.

Level 3. Each faculty member will have to determine if he or she has the power to change. He or she must ask, "Am I able to be open and honest in all my communications with this person? What about with that other person? What about with this group? What has kept me from being trustworthy in the past? Can I overcome that now?"

Level 4. Each person will have to ask, "How do I deal with a failure in trust, which is inevitable?"

Honest appraisals at all four levels require the opposite of self-justification and self-protection. Self-awareness at these four levels, therefore, requires a radical humility to be able to say, "I am apt to fail here. I have acted in ways that are not trustworthy in the past, and I may do so again." From such a humble stance, we can begin to ensure that our own communications are based on trust. When the inevitable happens, when one person in the organization withholds some relevant information or even lies, we can honestly acknowledge that we have done the same at one time. Furthermore, we may eventually begin to share our own personal testimonies about what it is like to have even one relationship in life absolutely based on trust. That is what Palmer (1998) means by living "a life divided no more."

Failing in Empowering Relationships

We borrowed from Kreisberg's (1992) definition of empowerment as "the ability to make a difference, to participate in decision making, and to take action for change" (p. xi). One of the suggestions made to foster empowering relationships in schools was to reexamine our notions of educational leadership. An application of Chouinard's (personal communication, July 11, 2003) four levels of dealing with failure in this area would look like this example:

Level 1. All educators must agree that educational leadership is not exclusively synonymous with administration.

Level 2. Faculty members will have to know when the expanded conception of leadership applies and when traditional notions of leadership should apply, that is, who makes what decisions and when.

Level 3. Each faculty member will have to decide if he or she has the power to change. He or she must ask, "Am I able to accept that in this school people other than appointed administrators will be empowered to lead?"

Level 4. Each person will have to ask, "How do I deal with a failure in this area of empowerment, which is bound to happen?"

Again, the humility should replace self-protection (of power and position) and self-justification (of actions). As one individual in the school is transformed from a *power over* stance to a *power with* stance, another individual may be transformed. It will be in face-to-face encounters and personal testimonies of failure and triumph that the organization will be slowly transformed.

Failing in Other-Centered Purposes

It is in this component of the Humane Dimension where self-disclosure and radical humility must prevail. To be other-centered in our schools means the following:

Level 1. All faculty members must agree that self-serving motives will not lead to school transformation.

Level 2. Faculty members will have to know when some self-serving motives will promote the agreed-on cause.

Level 3. Each person will have to determine if he or she has the power to move from a self-centeredness to other-centeredness.

Level 4. Each person will have to ask, "How do I deal with a failure in this vision of being other-centered?"

The work at each of these four levels takes incredible courage. It is so much easier to hide behind the images we have created of and for ourselves. The courage to move from one level to the next ultimately comes from knowing that there have been great people in our world who have been absolutely other-centered and, as a result, have helped transform the world.

Failing in Personal and Organizational Transformation

If public schools have failed in their efforts to reform education, then the potential for failure to transform education is inevitable. We view organizational transformation as part of a cycle that begins with personal transformation at an individual level. As explained in Chapter 5 on Personal and Organizational Transformation, this kind of change differs from reform in that it does the following:

- Stems from a deep and meaningful change in individual perspective
- Is more significant both to the development of the individual and, therefore, to the development of the organization
- Is characterized by a compassion for people
- Emanates from faith and not fear

Chouinard's (personal communication, July 11, 2003) four levels of dealing with a failure to transform could be exemplified as follows:

Level 1. All members of the group must agree that being transformed is significantly different from being reformed and that transformation begins within the individual.

Level 2. A conditional understanding of transformation will have to be articulated; for example, group members should discuss instances when reform must suffice.

Level 3. Each group member will have to examine how open, willing, and able he or she is to being transformed.

Level 4. Each individual must ask, "How will I deal with a failure in myself to be transformed?" In addition to this self-examination, individuals will have to inquire how they will deal with others in the organization who do not transform.

The language of faith certainly will aid in these conversations and reflections at each level.

FROM FACE-TO-FACE ENCOUNTERS TO CULTURAL CONNECTION

Transformation in education will begin as transformation *within* educators. This is the main point of our Humane Dimension. The kinds of changes described in our first seven chapters must originate in the heart and in the mind of one teacher, one administrator, one counselor, at a time. As these individuals begin to take on behaviors that have Other-Centered Purpose, for example, schools will slowly become places where Personal Transformation is allowed to occur. When a handful of teachers learns to Communicate in Trust, schools will become places where Personal Transformation is allowed to occur for other classroom teachers. The cycle of transformation is complete when two cultures connect. The final chapter that follows describes what evidence might exist for a newcomer in a school district to conclude that the Humane Dimension is present or not present.

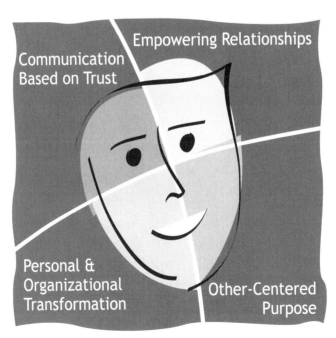

9

Evidence of the Humane Dimension in Schools

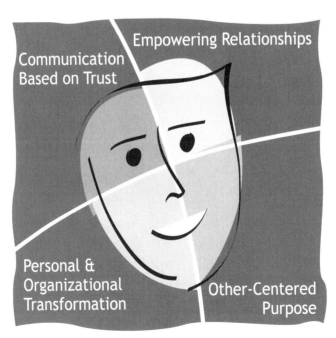

Humane Dimension

This book's closing thoughts to our readers are only the beginning. We say this because implementing the Humane Dimension starts with barely discernible differences in the ways we talk with and about each other. One-to-one encounters slowly begin to reflect genuine meaning. School programs undergo incremental transformation when members of a planning committee begin to trust each other's words and intentions. When one individual is empowered to take action for change, others observe *power with* put into action. One encounter, one meeting, one individual may only be the beginning, but it is the point of departure for a much needed cycle of transformation.

We have proposed throughout this book that organizational transformation is a process that begins with personal transformation. We have been careful to admit that our proposal is only a small part of the many efforts needed to improve public education. What we have provided is a context for transformation to occur. The *Humane Dimension*'s four elements, **Communication Based on Trust, Empowering Relationships, Other-Centered Purpose,** and **Personal and Organizational Transformation,** are four parts of a cycle. Each part can hardly stand alone and, instead, needs to be integrated with at least one of the other parts. This natural blending of elements does not prevent, however, our recognition of any one of them when present in our midst. With all our senses, we know when our communications with others is based on trust. We recognize an empowered individual. We can sense when other-centered purposes are enacted by how the well-being of the people involved is stressed. And we know, with our minds and our hearts, when transformation is unfolding before us.

There is evidence of the *Humane Dimension* in our daily lives. We asked six school practitioners to describe that evidence for our readers. These educators, from different levels of school life—an elementary principal, two middle school teachers, two high school principals, and one superintendent—were asked two questions:

1. If you were moving or changing jobs to another school district, what would be evidence to you that the elements of the Humane Dimension (i.e., Trust, Empowering Relationships, Other-Centered Purpose, and Personal Transformation) were present?

2. If you were moving or changing jobs to another school district, what would be evidence to you that the elements of the Humane Dimension were *not* present?

We believe our peers' responses will give clarity and direction for implementing the Humane Dimension. In addition to these responses, we offer concluding statements after each response to bring our own closure to their thoughts and to the book.

JEFF HARR, MIDDLE SCHOOL LANGUAGE ARTS TEACHER

The following is evidence that the elements of the Humane Dimension are present:

- Administrators wouldn't simply tell me what they wanted me to do; they'd want my input.
- They would ask me what I want rather than tell me what they need.
- They'd invite me to be a part of the decision-making process, right off the bat.
- Activities would be set up to take place before the school year began that would establish some relationships between the adults before the kids start showing up.
- A strong mentoring program for teachers new to the district would be established.
- Administrators would want to know more about me and less about how I run my classroom.
- Teachers and administrators would be talking, laughing, and enjoying each other's company.

The following is evidence that the elements of the Humane Dimension are *not* present:

- My first day of teaching would be the first time I would meet most of the staff.
- I'd hear many disparaging remarks from other teachers about the administration.
- I would work with lots of unhappy staff members.
- Micromanagement would be practiced.
- There would be an unhealthy focus on test scores, data, and the bottom line.
- Teachers would avoid their administrators.
- Students would walk right past their teachers in the hallway without smiling, saying hello, or in any way acknowledging their presence.

And This We Conclude . . .

- Teachers want to be included in decisions that directly affect their teaching and their students' learning.
- Relationship building is an important process in a teacher's life.
- Professional relationships and personal relationships are closely linked.
- Students mirror the attitudes of the adults in the building.

DONNA HESS, MIDDLE SCHOOL
LANGUAGE ARTS TEACHER

The following is evidence that the elements of the Humane Dimension are present:

- Interviews would take place with a group of people—teachers, administrators, possibly even students and parents.
- Questions during the interview would focus on intuitive and reflective aspects of teaching rather than on curricular and standards issues.
- The focus of the interview would be on the impact teachers have on the culture of the school and on students' lives.
- I would look at the relationship between the administration and the teachers' professional organization.
- A strong staff development program would be evident and would be an indication of the administration's support for and belief in the teachers of the district.
- The school system would encourage teachers to take risks and have innovative programs designed to meet the needs of the diverse school population.

The following is evidence that the elements of the Humane Dimension are *not* present:

- The school system would be very structured with many rules, guidelines, and procedures for teachers to follow, for example, a standard lesson plan form used by all teachers.
- The school system would not encourage much, if any, self-reflection on the part of teachers.
- There would be little, if any, shared decision making between teachers and administration.
- Learning would be "neat" and measurable," not "messy" and reflective.
- There would be little collaboration between teachers.

And This We Conclude . . .

- Promoting teacher reflection reveals a high regard for the teacher's role and responsibilities.
- Teachers should be recognized as instructional leaders as evidenced by their participation in the interview process.
- Masterful teaching does not look the same for all teachers.

ARDEN SOMMERS, HIGH
SCHOOL ASSISTANT PRINCIPAL

The following is evidence that the elements of the Humane Dimension are present:

- All staff members of the district would be able to articulate the mission of the district, not as a contrived statement, but in a conceptual framework that would indicate they truly understood the purpose of their work in that district.
- Professional meetings would frequently include membership from all areas of the staff, students, and community.
- Employment of new staff members would be a process where interviewing and input would include a cross section of the entire learning community.
- Evaluations of certified and classified staff members would be instruments for professional development; staff members would be the driving force for their own areas of improvement, with peers and administration as part of the team. The final product of this evaluation would come from the staff member.
- Staff members in leadership positions (principals, department chairs, central office, etc.) would view themselves as support members for instructional delivery, refraining from obtrusive interference and personal agendas.
- Discipline would be based on logical consequences and restitution rather than punitive measures.
- Mastery would be constant; time would be the variable.
- The teachers' association meetings would include discussions around professional development and teaching practices. Negotiations would be of a win/win nature.
- K–12 articulation and communication between all staff would be an expectation; central office would not only put structures in place for this to take place but would also remove any barriers that would prevent this.
- Conflict resolution would be the primary means of resolving issues within the organization.
- Adults would humble themselves to the needs of students.
- Student work would be considered in progress rather than finite.
- Students' input would be key to instructional and classroom design.
- Content would become a vehicle to higher-order thinking (problem solving, creativity, critical thinking, analysis, synthesis).
- Discussions around beliefs and vision would be ongoing to keep the vision clearly in sight.

The following is evidence that the elements of the Humane Dimension are *not* present:

- A clear mission/vision does not exist within the organization. A mission exists, but decisions are made arbitrarily based on personal agendas and political influence.
- Communication and articulation are poor; conflict and misunderstandings result.
- Students and staff are disenfranchised, resulting in lack of interest and motivation in teaching and learning.
- Leaders use their positions to fulfill Maslow's lower safety/security and belonging needs within themselves. The position then becomes a format for recognition, ladder climbing, and other self-interest needs.
- All members of the organization are in competition for what is perceived as limited power and resources.
- Because trust is low, the teachers' association would be primarily concerned with terms and conditions of employment. Negotiations would involve conflict and anger.
- The master schedule is done administratively, then held under strict security until its unveiling.

And This We Conclude . . .

- Principals must evaluate teachers for the primary purpose of promoting professional growth.
- The main responsibility of leaders should be to support and guide teachers in their designing engaging work for students.
- Information should be shared in an ongoing, fluid manner.

ROGER SIDOTI, HIGH SCHOOL PRINCIPAL

The following is evidence that the elements of the Humane Dimension are present:

Overt (Evident Through Simple Observation and Inquiry)

- Students and staff speak of their experiences at school using the words "our," "us," and so on. They speak of being happy and rarely criticize their experiences.
- On entering the building or district, everyone greets strangers with a smile and a positive expression of salutation.
- If on asking specific questions about an individual's work (who is an employee of the system), they respond in a passionate way, describing in some detail specifics about the work they are doing. This may be a teacher in the classroom, a superintendent, a secretary, a

custodian, or even a student. There is a sense of pride in what they are doing.

- Teachers view their administrators as colleagues, not adversaries. Principals speak of their staff, teachers, and support staff with respect and admiration.
- Although they may not agree to all the decisions made, parents are deeply respectful of the teachers, administrators, and support staff. They also know who people are by name and can describe a positive characteristic about them.
- Teachers volunteer their time and talents outside of the regular school day; administrators make it a priority to avoid the use of nonschool time.
- Teacher leaders refrain from being condescending to their teaching colleagues; teachers respect and support teacher leaders who are willing to step up and be proactive.
- Teachers are viewed as the experts and are given the latitude to design instructional strategies to improve student learning; they expect their principals to keep them informed about new strategies and concepts.
- Walking into the buildings of the district, you have a sense of lightness, positive energy, and a quiet hum of positive human interactions.
- There is evidence that students are part of the decision-making process. Just as our humanities class was a function of student leaders requesting the class, I would expect to hear from principals and teachers how students are given input in the decision-making process.
- I would see actions supporting the belief that "family comes first" for all employees and students, with colleagues stepping up to the plate to help one another. No one should ever have to make the decision between family and the school. School will keep!

Subtle (Evident Through Deeper Probing of Attitudes)

- All adults put their personal biases and egos aside. They realize that they do not have to personally like someone to follow a leader, and leaders know the value someone can bring to the organization even if they don't care for them personally.
- Leaders in the district welcome disagreement and encourage divergent thoughts. Followers respect the final decision made by the leader(s).
- Everyone feels that they can give input prior to a decision being made by the leader. They also understand it is input and some decisions rest on the leader's shoulders.
- Everyone understands the difference between personal power and positional power. The use of positional power is rare by the leader(s) in the district.

- People look at themselves relative to the organization. They understand how they fit into the big picture and what they contribute to the mission of the school.
- Being an educator is tough work. Everyone is honored, although they may be different in their styles. Teachers and principals celebrate these differences.
- Leaders are identified not solely on their ability to analyze data in decision making, but on their ability to use instinct.
- Principals respect teachers and design work for instructional growth not unlike how good classroom teachers design work for their students.
- Administrators are decisive and are unafraid to make "surgical strikes" in the organization if the circumstances warrant such action. Teachers give honest and forthright information about the decision through appropriate channels.
- Information is flowing within the organization.
- There is an understanding that consensus building means no one wants to take responsibility for a decision, especially when the leader is trying to build consensus. Rather, people are given the right to exercise freedom in problem solving through delegation, being praised when things go well, and being shielded from criticism when they do not by their leader, who takes responsibility for others' blunders.
- Aristotle's Golden Mean permeates the decision making within the district. Although people are passionate, they understand that moderation in all we personally do and say builds community. Extremes tear apart the fabric of school communities.
- People within the school community talk about their roles, regardless of their degrees, assignments, or status within the organization. They understand their roles and that there is little room for ego in the school community. It is replaced by a deep sense of responsibility, caring, and commitment that manifests itself in the actions of the vast majority of people within the school community.
- Regardless of formal position, the vast majority of school employees understand that they are leaders and must practice leadership.
- It is evident that the organization of the school system operates around the following: The superintendent serves the needs of his assistants in the central office; the central office personnel serve the needs of the principals; the principals serve the needs of their teachers; the teachers serve the needs of their students.
- The actions of administrators and teacher leaders are consistent with what they say they believe.
- Within the limitations of the complexities individual districts face, most people associated with the district are able to clearly identify the big concepts or beliefs the district stands for.

- Details are second to the big picture in all conversations, yet are clearly defined to meet specific objectives.
- It is clear that respect flows both ways, but it is the leader's responsibility to be respectful of everyone who allows him or her to lead. Leaders are respected less for their expertise (although important), but more for their character.
- I believe that the Humane Dimension places as much responsibility on followers as well as the leaders, and a synergy of excellence results when each acknowledges this truth and works to make this his or her personal practice.

And This We Conclude . . .

- Pride and passion about teaching and learning are fostered in a school climate characterized by caring relationships and adult communication.

- Discretionary uses of nonteaching time enhance personal and professional development.

- The same regard given to students for divergent thinking, individual needs, and decision making is given to the adults in the building.

DAVID BROBECK, SUPERINTENDENT

The following is evidence that the elements of the Humane Dimension are present:

- Various groups of teachers, administrators, parents, students, and community members would clearly describe the levels of trust, respect, purpose, and relationships in the district.
- The labor associations would be a good barometer of the relationships between the administration and the staff. Documentation of positive relationships would be found in meeting notes, newspaper articles, accounts of hearings, and so on.
- There is an understanding that the time it takes to evolve into a more humane dimension is long and arduous.

The following is evidence that the elements of the Humane Dimension are *not* present:

- Inquiries into the levels of trust, respect, purpose, and relationships in the district would reveal problems.

- Documentation of the relationships between the administration and labor associations would reveal years of distrust and contempt that have resulted in public skepticism.
- Individuals who operate in the Managerial Domain would be threatened by a move toward a more humane culture. They would react to a perceived loss of power with threats or coercion and become highly critical of colleagues who hold differing points of view.

And This We Conclude . . .

- Our work and our words in all aspects of school life reflect the presence or absence of the Humane Dimension.

- Moving toward a more Humane Dimension takes time and patience.

JOAN HOGREFE, ELEMENTARY PRINCIPAL

The following is evidence that the elements of the Humane Dimension are present:

- Everyone in the district is working as a team—not just in name but in actions. Actions that support the team concept must be present. Members of the team/district drive the reform, not just one individual. Their views are accepted and given serious consideration. Differences held by individuals are welcomed and sought.
- There is a feeling of family. One just knows if all is well when entering a building. The atmosphere is warm and inviting. People look, feel, and are genuinely happy. Even in the most difficult times, they know there is support among their peers and administrators. Each individual plays an important role in a building. There is value and respect for individuals, as these qualities impact the entire group.
- Trust is another trait that needs to be present. Individuals need to feel secure in that they can openly discuss an issue without worrying about fallout. With trust, individuals are willing to take risks. They want to do whatever it takes to make students successful. They will give of themselves without expecting anything in return. Academic achievement of students is a top priority, and scores reflect the efforts of the staff.
- Individuals speak openly and honestly about the previous evidence. They want others to know about their district and the individuals within the district. They are proud to be members of the district.

The following is evidence that the elements of the Humane Dimension are *not* present:

- Individuals are closed-minded to any new ideas. Things are done the way they have always been done with no attempt to change. All procedures must be rigidly followed. Academic achievement is low, and staff will not do anything to improve it.
- There is lack of respect for individuals. One would hear it in the comments made to others. The comments would be in the form of "put-downs."
- A "we versus they" atmosphere would exist. Unrest and considerable problems and grievances with teachers and classified staff would be a way of doing business. A top-down management style is present.
- Staff members would display a tired appearance. The energy level would be very low. A feeling of hopelessness would be evident. People would walk around without interacting with one another. They are just there to put in their time and leave.

And This We Conclude . . .

- Something "bigger than ourselves" looms pleasantly over individuals who operate in the Humane Dimension. This invisible presence includes space for dissent, allows room for risk taking, and generates hopeful energy.

- Within the Humane Dimension, actions and words are productive, optimistic, and constructive.

IN CLOSING . . .

The evidence of the Humane Dimension as reported by school practitioners repeats itself in varying forms. This cyclic nature of evidence mirrors the cyclic nature of the Humane Dimension itself. People trust each other. Individuals are empowered to make decisions. Individual intentions transcend personal motives and egotistical strivings. The organization transforms in harmony with the personal transformation of the people who live and work there.

We end this lengthy reflection on the Humane Dimension with a note written by Leslie Leonard to Roger Sidoti, principal of Roosevelt High School, a few months before her untimely death. The note itself is a powerful reminder that it is both human and humane to dwell in love.

In the spring of 2002, a panel of student leaders reflected on their senior year at Roosevelt to an audience of teachers and administrators.

One shared perception was the impact of the previous September 11 on their lives. The students discussed how the school had provided support and, at the same time, expressed a concern about their own futures in such uncertain times. Why, they wanted to know, couldn't there be some kind of course that would help them make sense of a world where terror of this nature could occur? Staff members asked the students to stay an hour longer than scheduled and together, they brainstormed what would eventually become the school's first humanities class. During the 2002–2003 school year, Leslie Leonard and Janice Hutchison designed the curriculum for the course that began in the fall of 2003. Within the first few weeks of her class, Leslie invited a panel of educators to speak with the humanities students. What follows is Leslie's letter thanking Roger Sidoti for speaking to the class.

September 28, 2003

Roger,

Many, many thanks for coming in to speak to the Humanities class with the panel and then returning to talk more with the students. I appreciate more than I can say your support of and openness with the Humanities concept. It's a wonderful journey that we're all on together!

And thank you, too, for always being a person with whom I can *share* power. I never feel like you try to have power *over* me, and thus I am more motivated to do my best, always being open to learn from you. I am so grateful for the chance you give me to be a true professional!

I hope you'll be able to visit 8th period more often. You are welcome any time.

Happy Fall,
Leslie

Resource A

Staff Development Activities for Component 1

Communication Based on Trust

Professional Development Notepad 1

Communication Based on Trust

Trust Fall

Procedures

1. No fall may be higher than four feet from the group.

2. Participants (catchers) must be assisted and spotted to the starting position with arms interlocked.

3. Each faller must have at least seven catchers (spotters). Additional catchers can be instructors, if required.

4. Catchers rotate to assume all spotting positions.

5. The catchers announce they are ready. Ready means hands in position, spotters looking at faller, paying attention.

SOURCE: Adapted from Adventure Education Center Instructor's Manual (Moore, 1993).

Professional Development Notepad 2

Communication Based on Trust

Trust Walk

The trust walk is designed for a staff retreat experience in the outdoors, such as at the Adventure Education Center in Columbus, Ohio. It teaches the importance of trusting another person.

Procedures

1. Find a partner.

2. Blindfold one of the pair, with the other being "the eyes" of the pair.

3. Select trail that has been scouted previously.

4. After one half of the walk is completed, partners change positions.

SOURCE: Adapted from Adventure Education Center Instructor's Manual (Moore, 1993).

Professional Development Notepad 3

Communication Based on Trust

Blade of Grass (Willow in the Wind)

The blade of grass exercise is designed for a staff meeting at any time of year. Its objective is to develop trust among participants.

Procedures

1. Have the group form a circle — the smaller the better.

2. Ask for a volunteer; explain the exercise, its safety commands, and its objectives.

3. The volunteer (in center of circle) folds arms across the chest and keeps the body rigid.

4. Using preparatory signals such as, Spotters ready? Ready! Falling! Fall on! The volunteer falls toward the spotting circle.

5. Those in the spotting circle will have hands up and will use a light-touch approach to the initial fall.

6. As the faller and the spotters gain confidence, the circle can enlarge so as to increase distance of the fall.

7. The faller can be returned to an upright position or can be passed around the circle, at the discretion of the group and faller.

SOURCE: Adapted from Adventure Education Center Instructor's Manual (Moore, 1993).

Professional Development Notepad 4

Communication Based on Trust

Lead Others as You Want to Be Led

People are willing to follow a leader because they have first been served by this leader. The demanding responsibilities placed on school leaders can create a sense of urgency and a sensation of compressed time. Getting the job done becomes paramount. To regain balance, leaders have to distinguish urgency from importance. They need to slow down. One way to do this is to recall how they want to be led.

Procedures

1. Regularly reflect on how it is you want to be led. Perhaps you can keep a weekly journal in which you describe leaders with whom you have worked. How did they bring out the best in you and in your peers? What did they do to inspire trust and build confidence?

2. Before and after an incident when you have been called on to lead, ask yourself, "How would I want to be led in a similar situation?"

Professional Development Notepad 5

Communication Based on Trust

Communication Is Not Telling

Meeting should provide varied opportunities for communications based on trust. A one-way dissemination of information is more efficiently (and effectively) accomplished through written formats like newsletters and bulletin board announcements. Some ways to enhance the trust among group members during meetings are listed:

Procedures

1. *Ask for input into meeting agendas.*

2. *Take turns leading discussions, perhaps by grade levels, departments, interests, and so on.*

3. *Whenever possible, include opportunities in meetings for small-group sharing.*

4. *Avoid simple dissemination of information.*

Professional Development Notepad 6

Communication Based on Trust

Discussing Student Work

Phil Schlechty's (2001) Center for Leadership in School Reform advocates an approach called the descriptive review process. This process encourages a nonjudgmental review and discussion about samples of completed student work. The goal is not to evaluate the teacher. The goal is to enhance communication about the work teachers design for students. The following are some ways to encourage similar, non-threatening conversations:

Procedures

1. At various meetings throughout the school year, ask teachers to bring in samples of completed student work. These meetings can be faculty meetings, grade-level meetings, department meetings, and so on.

2. Arrange people in small groups of no more than seven or eight individuals, with one member of each group sharing his or her students' work.

3. Before anyone can speak, ask the group members to examine the student work. Then they can share their observations and questions about the work. It is important that observations and questions are not criticisms. Instead, they are to reflect on the kind of work the students are doing and the levels of student engagement engendered by the work.

4. The teacher then responds to the group's comments and questions.

5. The groups end with a sharing of what-ifs and how-abouts aimed at extending student thinking and engagement even more.

Professional Development Notepad 7

Communication Based on Trust

Confident Expectations

To trust someone means to expect confidently, to expect the truth from that person. At the beginning of a school initiative, people need to expect confidently that the leaders will support their work. In the middle of a school initiative, people need to expect the truth about their work from the leaders. Leaders do not have to guess what these expectations are; they can just ask.

Procedures

1. At critical phases throughout a school initiative, circulate expectation forms. On these forms, ask the individuals who are carrying out the initiative to list what they expect from the leader(s). These expectations may include responses such as time to plan, input into budget decisions, a role in the evaluation design, and so on.

2. Be sure each expectation form is signed. After all, trust must be reciprocal.

3. Through private conversations, check in with each individual to discuss the expectations. Are they being met? If not, what kinds of changes should be made?

Resource B

Staff Development
Activities for Component 2

Empowering Relationships

Professional Development Notepad 1

Empowering Relationships

Seeing the Bigger Picture

Understanding the whole child in the classroom means understanding what he or she has learned in previous years and what he or she will learn in the next few years. An enhanced sense of both what students learn and how they learn it (i.e., an expanded notion of curriculum and instruction through the school years) helps teachers and administrators reconnect "school parts" that have traditionally been separated by grade groupings.

Procedures

1. As districtwide courses of study are being written, arrange triads of teachers and administrators who represent early grades, the middle grades, and the high school. Each team member visits the other two levels and observes the enactment of that particular curricular area. Observations should focus on lesson and unit objectives as well as on learning activities.

---

2. Team members write reflections about their observations with particular emphasis on implications for their own grade-level instruction.

3. Some teams may be encouraged to design collaborative units of instruction. Partner research could be conducted through e-mail communications.

4. Teams may also analyze standardized test results to determine areas of strengths and weaknesses. Gaps in student learning can be and should be addressed in nontesting years as well.

Professional Development Notepad 2

Empowering Relationships

Creation of Order Through Open Investigations

A creation of order will require both personal and professional courage. One small step toward a creation of order in which educators carry on adult conversations could be accomplished with open investigations into how power relations are affecting specific school programs, decisions, plans, and so on.

Procedures

1. The individuals closest to the decision should be the very ones engaged in the conversations about the decision. Identifying all key stakeholders is the first step in opening up communication.

2. Once all the key people are included in the conversation, a creation of order should be declared. The group's facilitator can begin by describing the traditional need for order that has prevented an open exchange of ideas and opinions. The facilitator can then describe an alternative—the creation of order in which participants openly investigate how power relations are affecting a particular program, decision, plan, and so on.

3. Each participant is asked to complete a power grid by identifying on paper the types of power the other participants wield in the enactment of the program or decision being discussed. Types of power might include hiring, scheduling, planning, and controlling resources.

4. Once the various types of power have been identified and openly discussed, the participants will describe how the uses of those powers affect the program. Both positive and negative effects should be openly described. The facilitator will have to be sensitive to the potential of hurt feelings when negative effects are brought out in the conversation.

Professional Development Notepad 3

Empowering Relationships

1,000 Words (Informal Observations)

Adult learning is strengthened by observations of actual practice. Because many teachers have limited opportunities to watch their peers teach, opening the classroom doors for informal observations can be empowering experiences for both the observer and the observed.

Procedures

1. Establish a focus for the observations based on staff development goals, instructional concerns, curricular aims, and so on. Some foci could include the following:

   Asking questions at higher levels of information
   Using technology for delivery of information
   Collecting anecdotal evidence of student learning
   Differentiating instruction

2. Design a simple observation form that highlights the focus. For instance, if the focus is asking questions at higher levels of cognition, the form would include space to list teacher questions and to identify the levels of cognition.

3. Elicit volunteers to observe and to be observed.

4. Schedule the observations. Be sure to balance the load of peer observation by using some nonteaching time and by providing coverage.

5. Provide opportunities for sharing feedback. This could take place at the beginning or the end of a faculty meeting.

Professional Development Notepad 4

Empowering Relationships

It's Not All Black and White

Too often, we evaluate ourselves and others by identifying what was good and what was bad about a lesson, a meeting, a program, and so on. Although such an approach helps us sort through myriad components and interactions, it is only an *initial step toward making a difference. Empowerment results when we reflect more deeply in a way that transcends more praise and blame.*

Procedures

1. *Observer: What are some things (note the plural ending) you did to help the students learn? (Encourage the teacher to expand on the response. Ask for more than initially provided.)*

2. *Observer: How do you know that these things helped the students learn? (This type of question encourages the teacher to recollect evidence of learning.)*

3. *Observer: If you could teach this lesson over again, what would you do differently to help the students learn even more? Why?*

NOTE: The above procedure reflects a conversation between a teacher and an observer (peer or principal). Similar exchanges can be used, with modification, in a reflective conversation about meetings, programs, and so on.

Professional Development Notepad 5

Empowering Relationships

Empowering to Solve Problems

People who do not feel empowered in an organization often confuse criticism with critical thinking. For example, they may confuse complaining with constructive criticism or the reporting of problems with leadership. One way to empower individuals is to encourage them to brainstorm solutions to the problems they identify.

Procedures

1. *Get the message out that identifying a problem is the first step in problem solving.*

2. *Encourage individuals to accompany reports of problems in the school with possible solutions.*

3. *Consider brainstorming additional solutions with the individual.*

Professional Development Notepad 6

Empowering Relationships

Share the Load; Share the Lead

Meetings are a major part of organizational life. Although some meetings probably should never take place because they function merely to deliver information (a task that is more efficiently accomplished with a memo), other meetings serve a vital role. Ideas are developed through brainstorming. Adult communication is modeled. Group deliberation is enhanced. Relationships can be empowered by sharing the responsibility for facilitating meetings. The following process can help, especially if one person typically facilitates a group's meetings.

Procedures

1. Identify one or two group members who may have a particular interest in the group's work.

2. Before finalizing the meeting agenda, ask those individuals for input. What else might they include on the agenda? What kinds of group activities would generate discussion? Would they like to lead those activities during the meetings?

3. After the meeting, ask them for feedback. What occurred during the meeting that led to good discussion, positive action, and so on? What could be done differently?

4. Eventually, share the lead in the meeting designs and enactment.

Professional Development Notepad 7

Empowering Relationships

Decision-Making Strategies

Having to guess at how decisions are made can weaken individual resolve and commitment. Yet when people know the process of decision making, it is not just individual resolve and commitment that are strengthened. Personal and professional trust is strengthened as well.

Procedures

1. Identify typical areas of decision making in your district and school. Examples could include hiring, evaluation, curriculum development, and staff development.

2. Create a graphic overview that clearly details how the decisions are made in each area. Who is involved? At what level in the decision-making process are these individuals involved? What criteria are considered? Who is responsible for the final decision? How is feedback gathered and included?

3. After decisions are made, use the graphic overview to chart how clearly the decision-making design was followed.

Resource C

Staff Development
Activities for Component 3

Other-Centered Purpose

Professional Development Notepad 1

Other-Centered Purpose

Case Method

"This learning device is used by a leader to anticipate and interpret the other person's perspective" (Argyris, 1999b).

Procedures

1. *In one paragraph, describe a key organizational problem as you see it.*

2. *Assume you could talk to whomever you wish to begin to solve the problem. Describe, in a paragraph or so, the strategy that you would use in this meeting.*

3. *Next, split your page into two columns. On the right-hand side, write how you would begin the meeting—what you would actually say. Then write what you believe the other(s) would say. Then write your response to their response. Continue writing this scenario for two or so double-spaced typewritten pages.*

4. *In the left-hand column, write any idea or feeling that you would have that you would not communicate for whatever reason. (p. 134)*

Professional Development Notepad 2

Other-Centered Purpose

The Talking Circle

This method of communication has been used by Native Americans for thousands of years. Its objectives are to elicit open and honest communication and to learn to listen to what others are saying (Manitonquat, 2004).

Procedures

1. Line up chairs in a circle so all can see each other.

2. If the group is large, divide it into several circles.

3. The facilitator may ask someone from the group to be a recorder.

4. The facilitator begins by discussing the history of talking circles and the objective of bringing people into the presence of each other.

5. The facilitator emphasizes the importance of the collective point of view and that all things concluded must be for the good of the group (Struthers, 2002).

6. Initial group discussions should be focused on shared values, beliefs, and commitments.

7. The facilitator eventually uses the recorded comments to give feedback outside of the talking circle.

Professional Development Notepad 3

Other-Centered Purpose

The Talking Stick

This method is introduced by a facilitator as a listening and speaking methodology that is transformative (Fujioka, 1998). Its objective is to encourage all participants to speak their minds during the meeting and to focus attention on others.

Procedures

1. Like the talking circle, the talking stick occurs in a circle of chairs.

2. The facilitator begins by recalling the Native American's belief that the stick was imbued with spiritual qualities that called up the spirit of the ancestors to guide good decisions.

3. After introducing the concept, the facilitator passes the stick to a participant in the circle; a topic may or may not be specified by the facilitator.

4. Whoever is holding the stick is asked to speak from the heart (Fujioka, 1998).

5. Others are not to speak but also are not to think ahead about what they are going to say; rather, they are to concentrate on the speakers' words.

6. No one is allowed to comment on what another has said.

7. All are given a chance to speak.

Professional Development Notepad 4

Other-Centered Purpose

Respectful Use of Time

One way that we can demonstrate our regard for others is through a respectful use of time in our organizations. We know this, yet how often does time slip away at meetings because of a late start or a poorly planned agenda? It has been said that "common sense is not common." What follows is a reminder of what many already know.

Procedures

1. Pay careful attention in meetings facilitated by others. Does the session begin and end on time? How much time is devoted to certain items? Develop your own sense of timing, just as good classroom teachers do, so you can predict, as far as possible, how long certain agenda items will take.

2. Announce at the beginning of the meeting that you will start on time and end on time. Then do it. People will develop a confident expectation in the area of your leadership.

Professional Development Notepad 5

Other-Centered Purpose

Appreciative Inquiry on Purpose

According to the developers of appreciative inquiry (AI), Cooperrider and Whitney (1999), "Human systems grow toward what they persistently ask questions about" (p. 10). Individuals and, therefore, organizations are transformed by capacities. At the building level, an appreciative inquiry of purpose could look something like this:

Procedures

1. *Identify one or two building movements such as a new program, curriculum innovations, changed positions, and so on.*

2. *Explain to the faculty that these areas will be examined for their capacity to enhance the school's culture.*

3. *Write two interview questions for each school movement to be examined. A general approach to writing these questions is that Question 1 evokes what evidence shows the positive capacity of the movement and Question 2 generates suggestions for growth.*

4. *Establish an interview schedule. (Each interview will take about 30 minutes.) All faculty members should be interviewed. One way to complete the interviews may be to have 5 to 15 volunteers interview the rest of the faculty over the course of six weeks. Another way would be to have one half of the faculty interview the other half during a faculty meting. At the next meeting, the roles would be reversed.*

   > *Example: Student Advocacy Program*
   >
   > *Question 1: Describe a time when you have seen a student benefit from the advocacy program. What did people do to help the student(s)?*
   >
   > *Question 2: In what ways can the student advocacy program be changed to help students even more?*

NOTE: The questions are framed in such a way as to focus on the purpose of student support.

Professional Development Notepad 6

Other-Centered Purpose

Compassion for People Versus Passion for a Topic

Topic: Standardized Test Scores

What can be a dogged pursuit of improving student test scores through ongoing data analysis and alignment of standards with instructional and assessment practices can become a humane experience when the whole child and the whole teacher are both taken into consideration.

Procedures

Teachers should be regularly surveyed to find out what supports their efforts at improving test scores and what constrains their efforts. The following are two questions that could be posed to faculty members:

1. What practices, policies, and procedures currently support your work in standards-based education?

2. What practices, policies, and procedures currently constrain your work in standards-based education?

Resource D

Staff Development
Activities for Component 4

Personal and Organizational Transformation

Professional Development Notepad 1

Personal and Organizational Transformation

Telling Our Stories

A basic premise of appreciative inquiry (AI) is that "human systems grow toward what they persistently ask questions about" (Cooperider & Whitney, 1999, p. 10). If we want to create schools where students are challenged intellectually, we should ask questions about when, how, and why that has happened in the life of the school.

Procedures

1. Allow time for this storytelling process to take place. This is not a faculty meeting activity that begins and ends on time in an afternoon session.

2. Ask for a group of volunteers from the faculty to read Cooperrider and Whitney's (1999) booklet on AI so that they can understand AI's potential and process.

3. Ask the group to create a set of questions related to the school's vision. For example, pairs of questions can be asked. Such questions could include the following:

      a. Think of a time when some of your students were really challenged intellectually. What did they do? How were they supported in their intellectual growth?

      b. What else could we be doing at our school to enhance the intellectual development of all our students?

4. The group then develops an interview schedule, allowing approximately 45 minutes to interview each faculty member.

5. An analysis of the responses is conducted for shared comments, themes, and so on.

6. The questions could also be rewritten for parent and student interviews.

SOURCE: Adapted from Appreciative Inquiry (Cooperrider & Whitney, 1999).

Professional Development Notepad 2

Personal and Organizational Transformation

Literature Review and Action Research

Action research is a viable way of directly addressing professional doubts. An important step in the action research process is the literature review. This phase typically occurs after researchers identify an area of their practice that has proven to be problematic. Before any researcher chooses which interventions to try out, a review of professional literature should be conducted. Action researchers who work in small study groups have found that sharing their findings brings clarity and direction to their research.

Procedures

1. Most action researchers rely on three main sources of professional literature: online databases, visits to a university library, and professional organizations.

2. Members of an action research group should plan on spending four to six weeks apart while the literature is being accessed and reviewed. During this review time, researchers should be encouraged to keep track of the themes in the literature as well as important ideas for practice.

3. On regrouping, the researchers should begin to share their literature reviews. The group facilitator could request brief summaries of each piece of literature read. These summaries might include bibliographic information, key findings, and suggestions for practice. Future action researchers in the building or district will be able to use this collection of professional literature reviews.

Professional Development Notepad 3

Personal and Organizational Transformation

A Culture of Civility

Humans thrive in a culture of civility, a culture characterized by acts of kindness, genuine concern for the individual, and authentic admissions of wrong. Thank you, I am so sorry, and I was wrong are sincere expressions meant to mend and not to excuse incivility. Fostering a culture cannot depend solely on company mandates or district slogans. Civility begins with one face-to-face encounter and moves to another face-to-face encounter, from personal transformation to organizational transformation.

Procedures

1. Servant-leaders model civility when they overcome a fear of appearing weak by admitting they may be wrong or that they made a mistake. In so doing, they empower those around them to take risks because they have demonstrated that mistakes occur and can be overcome.

2. Public apologies and public thank-you's can be even more powerful than private exchanges.

Professional Development Notepad 4

Personal and Organizational Transformation

Listening With the Heart

The rapid pace of school life often leaves us with little time to do more than offer advice to colleagues who share their concerns with us. We jump in with suggestions. We sympathize with their plights. We affirm their criticisms of others. These responses do little to transform. Instead, we can learn to listen for what is not being said.

Procedures

Questions and comments like these can help us listen with our hearts:

1. What do you want this to look like?

2. What concerns you the most about this?

3. What do you need to take place?

4. What is the worst that can happen here?

5. How can I help?

6. What do you need me to do to help?

7. Why does this worry you?

8. In five years, how might you feel about this?

9. Why might _____ (name) be reacting this way?

10. Could there be another way to look at this?

Professional Development Notepad 5

Personal and Organizational Transformation

Go to the Person Who Has Offended You

There is a saying that aptly addresses much of our personal discontent: We make ourselves suffer just as much when we take offense as when we give it. We suffer as we ruminate on the offense; then we spread the pain by discussing the offense with another (and another, and perhaps, another). An alternative approach than can heal and strengthen is to go to the person who has offended us.

Procedures

1. Instead of discussing your feelings with another individual not connected to the offensive event or remark, go directly to the person who is responsible for your discomfort, anger, pain, and so on.

2. Privately and politely express your feelings. The intent here is to engage in conversation, not to blame or to chastise. Words that can open up a conversation are gentle and nonaccusatory; they may sound like this:

   I've been thinking about the comment you made in our meeting this morning when you said that I "tore through" the presentation to the department chairs last week. Do you think I should have taken more time with the presentation? I had some reasons for working quickly, and I'd like to have a conversation about this with you.

3. Let the conversation be a conversation and not an argument.

Professional Development Notepad 6

Personal and Organizational Transformation

Time to Grow

Personal development that leads to organizational transformation takes time. In order for a new program to flourish, thoughtful planning should be encouraged. Likewise, reflective practice and program evaluation should be fostered.

Procedures (for Fostering the Developing of a New Program)

1. *Once an innovation has been thoughtfully considered (i.e., a needs assessment has been conducted and impact on the organization has been considered), the program leader should be given time to plan. For at least one semester, one period each day should be set aside for the individual to plan the program. Details such as schedules, curriculum, materials, and so on can be worked out during this time. Collaborative relationships within the school and between the school and the community can be established. This time will help ensure both the program's successes and the individual's development.*

2. *Once the program begins, establish a schedule of review sessions with the program leader. During these sessions, the program leader can work with others to assess the program's strengths and weaknesses and to brainstorm further directions.*

Professional Development Notepad 7

Personal and Organizational Transformation

Multiple Perspectives

When we become capable of taking on multiple perspectives of an event or of a person, we move beyond the flatness of our presuppositions and learn to relate. Seeing events and people through others' eyes is not easy nor is it comfortable. Providing opportunities to develop multiple perspectives, however, can reduce the threat of change and enhance growth.

Procedures

1. *Establish stations around the room where stakeholders of an event meet to discuss the program, class, and so on. Each station should represent the*

vantage points of various individuals. For example, stations may be labeled Board of Education, Superintendent, Special Education Students, Elementary Teachers, Parents, and so on. Have chart paper and markers at each station.

2. Separate the individuals in the room into small groups so that there is one group for each station. Instruct the groups to brainstorm on the chart paper the opinions they believe that particular individual or clusters of individuals would have about the event. How might the Superintendent see this program? What might he or she be concerned about? Why might he or she want to see it prosper?

3. After about 10 minutes, ring a bell and instruct the groups to move clockwise to the next station. Continue this process until each group has had a chance to brainstorm at each station.

4. Debrief on the process by asking people to share how their perspectives have been changed since coming into the room.

Resource E

Adventure Education Center

Overview

THE PROGRAM

The Adventure Education Center located in Columbus, Ohio, is a multisite regional outdoor adventure education center serving hundreds of schools and agencies throughout Ohio. It was formed in 1982 and is a program of Direct Instructional Support Systems (D.I.S.S.), Inc., a nonprofit educational organization. Dr. Gary K. Moore leads the center's efforts.

Since its beginning, the center and its network have served more than 40,000 central Ohio youth and adults. The center offers a variety of activities: youth leadership conferences, summer camp opportunities for youth, substance abuse prevention programs, and a variety of staff development activities for both schools and corporations.

The model by which the program operates involves area practitioners who become actively involved as instructors. These instructors receive their training through the Leadership Series in Experiential Education, a program of D.I.S.S. Throughout the year, national, regional, and local leaders in the field of experiential education provide workshops in a variety of activities. Most workshops are held on weekends and during the summer. Participants receive graduate and undergraduate credit from a consortium of area colleges and universities and come from a variety of backgrounds: physical education teachers, classroom teachers, youth leaders, guidance counselors, and recreation professionals. Once trained, these instructors provide a pool of staff to meet the demands for the center's programs, while at the same time having positive implications for school-community curriculums. Our eventual goal is for these instructors to become trainers who will eventually train others in their school or agency. The networking taking place within this workshop format has proven to be a very effective tool for not only in building the programs of the center but also in creating cohesiveness among teachers and others looking to share new ideas. Furthermore, networking informs the staff of accepted peer practice within the field of outdoor adventure education.

PROGRAM OPTIONS

A majority of those who use the facilities at the Adventure Education Center incorporate their curriculum into the programs. We've listed some of those ways members of the network take advantage of the tailor-made activities.

1. *An eight-hour activity period consisting of a ground-level teambuilding initiative experience and a high-level ropes course experience.*

2. *A modified day with activity periods plus additional staff to provide maximum activity time.* This format enables the group to receive both a low- and high-element experience. A group of 120 participants is the maximum number permitted. Additional staff is required to facilitate these numbers. We usually assign an extra instructor to the ropes course. It is possible to schedule this experience from 8:30 A.M. to 2:30 P.M.

3. *A four-hour activity period with a large group of participants (50–100).* This format has been proven to be most successful because of its flexibility in working within the school schedule. This format allows a special area teacher (physical education, guidance counselor) to bring a large number of students without having to provide the employment of a substitute teacher to cover classes at school. It is not uncommon to have eight to ten groups on the initiative course at one time. With the large number of low-element activity areas, a rotation schedule provides easy access to a variety of challenges. Many of the low elements have been duplicated in several locations throughout the site. With the construction of our fifth high-ropes course, a group of 72 could participate within the four hours; however, we recommend that groups scheduling the use of a high element have preliminary experiences with new games, group challenges, or cooperative games and sports. The activity packet the group leader receives prior to the scheduled event contains a sample of these activities. Because of transportation logistics, the most popular times are 9:30 A.M. to 1:30 P.M. This allows travel time to and from school plus an on-site picnic lunch.

4. *The modified 24-hour experience in which the group arrives in late afternoon and spends the night in a primitive cabin.* Group size is limited to 24 participants. This format allows ample time to deal with some specific

issues or just for the fun of it. The group begins with ice-breakers and low-level initiative activities until late evening. This is followed by dinner and a late-night high-element ravine crossing until 11:00 P.M. The following morning begins with a high-ropes-course experience concluding with a debriefing and departure at noon.

In addition, groups of 100 have used the low-level initiative course in the early evening followed by the overnight at a nearby resident camp. Quest programs have used this format to build on the peer counseling aspect of the program. The Worthington High School in Worthington, Ohio, is another program that combines exciting activities with specific objectives for substance abuse prevention education.

5. *Weekend or three-day retreats have become increasingly popular.* Model programs have been developed in cooperation with the following:

- *Worthington High School.* A three-day adventure-based substance abuse program for high school coaches, advisors, students, and athletes. Activities in addition to the on-site offerings include waterskiing, sailing, board sailing, indoor climbing wall, shooting sports, and scuba diving.
- *Fostoria High School, Fostoria, Ohio.* A weekend retreat for their school Quest classes. This program consists of popular on-site activities and selected off-site programming.

6. *Sometimes it better serves a group to take the activities to a location other than the Adventure Education Center.* Many portable initiatives are available to meet this need.

Resource F

A Generic Process of
Procedures for Win/Win

FIRST SESSION: SELECTION OF AN
EXPERIENCED WIN/WIN FACILITATOR

Prior to the initial planning meeting, both sides or teams must select an experienced, professional facilitator (and cofacilitator, if the budget allows). Both sides must agree to equally share the cost of these services. Although the role of the facilitator is implied in each of the following steps, we note here several purposes of this professional in win/win negotiations. The facilitator brings to the bargaining table a neutral, third-party professional's point of view. Having no direct stake in either side's point of view, he or she has the freedom to move arguments forward from either side and to prevent inertia or impasse from setting in to the process bringing clarity and definition when either side is unable to see it or articulate it. Overtly, the facilitator keeps track of who has just spoken, who has requested to speak next by a show of hand, and who has requested to speak after that, and in this manner, the facilitator chooses who has the floor to speak. The facilitator is a process observer who ensures that rules, regulations, and guidelines that were developed by the group at the initial planning meeting (see next step) are followed and not violated. The cofacilitator takes copious notes from the first moment to the last, so that the principal facilitator may interject and reflect with the whole group any prior discussion or argument that might be germane to the current debate. The facilitator also helps the group to ascertain that it has just agreed to a proposal, that the actual wording is acceptable to all, and that any final resolutions are prepared and typed in a format to which all can agree after each session when resolutions occur. Finally, the facilitator is responsible for arranging specific details of location, food, schedules, and so on after these details had been discussed at the initial planning meeting (see next step).

SECOND SESSION: INITIAL PLANNING MEETING

Both sides or negotiating teams must meet with a trained win/win facilitator at an initial planning meeting. At this meeting, the following activities should occur: (a) a review of and agreement on materials covering rules, roles, and regulations to be used; (b) the selection of a neutral site and physical arrangements to be employed for interactions; (c) the identification of participants to represent both sides; (d) the determination of timeline, such as dates and times for the bargaining sessions; (e) an inservice and orientation on the nature of win/win, its solutions, and consensus building; and (f) the preparation of the agenda for the next meeting.

THIRD SESSION: INFORMATION SHARING

Several points must be stressed in the first session. First, *voluntary participation* must be emphasized, and either side must understand that it has the right to withdraw from the process at any time and to return to conventional bargaining should a team's members become dissatisfied with win/win negotiations. Second, win/win philosophy and psychology should be reviewed and emphasized. Third, each side shares any general information or background that might help the other side to understand the issues and concerns that will be raised. Fourth and finally, with the guidance of the facilitator, both sides move into an activity of listing all questions that have emerged from each team's issues or concerns. An example here might be beneficial. Consider a question raised by the team representing the board of education: "How can we continue to offer excellent health insurance to all employees and, at the same time, to limit the rising costs of health care?" Typically, all questions are posted on chart paper around the room's wall space. (When the wording of an issue or concern becomes awkward in the form of a question, a statement may be used in rare cases.)

FOURTH SESSION: PRIORITIZING
QUESTIONS, ISSUES, AND CONCERNS

We advise the reader here that our descriptions of sessions may overlap previous or subsequent sessions; that is, the flow of good communication must not be hampered by artificial borders or lock-step procedures per session. Assuming that both sides presented their exhaustive list of questions during the first session, we recommend next that questions be prioritized and that these issues and concerns be addressed in the order of most important to least important. In addition, the group must determine whether or not some questions are site specific; oftentimes, these site-specific questions may be deferred to a plan and schedule for resolving them. In the next step, "Win/Win Step 3: Decision Making and Reviewing Through Dialogue Sessions," we suggest how follow-up dialogue sessions (i.e., after the contract is settled) may be used to address site-specific issues that need resolution but that do not belong in a teachers' contract.

The groups also must determine if questions already have been addressed deliberately or inadvertently before negotiations begin. If the issue already has been addressed, it should be discarded immediately, as appropriate.

Furthermore, all agenda items must be reviewed for their need to be resolved before a contract may be written. Specifically, if an item does not need to be included in the contract, then it should be deferred to discussion at dialogue sessions that follow the contract's signing.

The final activity for this session and every other session is to set the agenda for the next meeting. To avoid agenda overloading, Crisci and Herpel (1984) recommend that agenda items (i.e., questions, issues, and concerns) be evaluated on the basis of: (a) the problem's impact on all the groups represented, (b) the problem's need for integration of the views of all constituents, (c) the potential for the problem's solution to benefit everyone, and (d) fiscal and legal implications of the problem. Also, where applicable, agenda items should be combined and coalesced if they represent like concerns from both sides.

FIFTH SESSION: ADDRESSING QUESTIONS, ISSUES, AND CONCERNS IN PRIORITY ORDER

The group meets to discuss those questions, issues, and concerns identified at the previous session by the group as the highest priority. Each side must come prepared to provide information that is germane to each question or agenda item. During this and subsequent working sessions, statements of concern about the question are shared. In addition, possible solutions are generated with an emphasis on consensus, not compromise. This fifth session remains the format for all subsequent sessions other than the final session.

The focus of these working sessions is to agree on concepts. The following three important steps occur in a recursive cycle. First, smaller groups or subcommittees, with representatives from both sides, may be needed to work through the details of a particular concept between sessions. Second, the whole group (i.e., both sides) later reviews the presentations of subcommittees and, for that matter, reviews all other concepts with the intention of agreeing conceptually to a solution. Third, the whole group may be divided into writing subcommittees to move a resolution from conceptual form to contract format. This third step is the primary means of developing preliminary contract provisions. Ultimately, the whole group must review and approve (i.e., tentatively agree to) each provision.

FINAL SESSION: AGREEING TO THE FINAL CONTRACT LANGUAGE

Because each provision is agreed to only tentatively, there is no final agreement on each or any of these provisions until the group comes to agreement on all provisions assembled together in a final contract. After final agreement occurs, each side must present the recommended contract to their respective governing/voting bodies. After both bodies agree to the entire contract by vote, both sides formally sign the negotiated agreement.

At this final session, both sides must determine the process and schedule for the ongoing communications forum that must occur throughout the year. As minor as these dialogue sessions may seem after the celebration of successful contract negotiations, these ongoing communications are critical for several reasons, to include: avoiding the use of the grievance procedure, resolving matters deferred at the collective-bargaining table to dialogue sessions, clarifying any matters related to implementing new contract language, and creating a forum for addressing new issues and concerns that arise.

References and Suggested Readings

Argyris, C. (1999a). Making knowledge more relevant to practice: Maps for action. In E. E. Lawler, A. M. Mohrman, S. A. Mohrman, G. E. Ledford, & T. G. Cummings (Eds.), *Doing research that is useful for theory and practice* (pp. 79–107). New York: Lexington Books.

Argyris, C. (1999b). Tacit knowledge and management. In R. J. Sternberg & J. A. Horvath (Eds.), *Tacit knowledge in professional practice* (pp. 123–140). Mahwah, NJ: Erlbaum.

Argyris, C. (2001). Good communication that blocks learning. In *Harvard business review on organizational learning* (pp. 87–109). Boston: Harvard Business School.

Astuto, T. A., Clark, D. L., Read, A., McGree, K., & Fernandez, L. P. (1994). *Roots of reform: Challenging the assumptions that control change in education.* Bloomington, IN: Phi Delta Kappa Educational Foundation.

Autry, J. A. (2002). *The servant leader.* Sacramento, CA: Prima.

Avolio, B. J., & Bass, B. M. (Eds.). (2002). *Developing potential across a full range of leadership.* Mahwah, NJ: Erlbaum.

Baatz, C. A. (1980). *The philosophy of education: A guide to information sources.* Detroit, MI: Gale Research Company.

Barnhart, C. L. (Ed.). (1951). *The American college dictionary.* New York: Random House.

Barwick, J. T. (1990). Team building: A faculty perspective. *Community College Review, 17*(4), 33–39.

Beane, J. (1991). Middle school: The natural home of integrated curriculum. *Educational Leadership, 49,* 9–13.

Belenky, M. F., Clinchy, B. M., Goldberger, N. R., & Tarule, J. M. (1986). *Women's ways of knowing.* New York: Basic Books.

Berliner, D., & Biddle, B. (1995). *The manufactured crisis: Myths, fraud, and the attack on America's public schools.* Reading, MA: Addison-Wesley.

Blake, R. R., & Mouton, J. S. (1964). *The managerial grid.* Houston, TX: Gulf.

Blanchard, K., Carlos, J. P., & Randolph, A. (1996). *Empowerment takes more than a minute.* San Francisco: Berrett-Koehler.

Bloom, B. (1956). *Taxonomy of educational objectives, Handbook I: Cognitive domain.* New York: David McKay.

Bolman, L. G., & Deal, T. E. (1995). *Leading with soul: An uncommon journey of spirit.* San Francisco: Jossey-Bass.

Bolman, L. G., & Deal, T. E. (1997). *Reframing organizations: Artistry, choice, and leadership*. (2nd ed.). San Francisco: Jossey-Bass.

Bracey, G. (1997). The seventh Bracey report on the condition of public education. *Phi Delta Kappan, 79*(2), 120–136.

Brobeck, D. G. (1998). *Assessing the impact of interventions on the Cardinal Administrator Interview for principal selection*. Unpublished doctoral dissertation, Kent State University, Kent, Ohio.

Brooks, J., & Brooks, M. (1993). *The case for constructivist classrooms*. Alexandria, VA: Association for Supervision and Curriculum Development.

Bruner, J. (1965). In defense of verbal learning. In R. C. Anderson & D. P. Ausubel (Eds.), *Readings in the psychology of cognition*. New York: Holt, Rinehart & Winston.

Calhoun, E. F. (2002). Action research for school improvement. *Educational Leadership, 59*, 18–24.

Candoli, C. (1991). *School system administration: A strategic plan for site based management*. Lancaster, PA: Technomic.

Cardinal, K. (1985). *Administrator interview*. Kent, OH: Ken Cardinal & Associates.

Chapman, J. (Ed.). (1990). *School based decision making and management*. London: Falmer Press.

Check, J. W. (1997, May/June). Teacher research as powerful professional development. *The Harvard Education Letter*.

Cherryholmes, C. H. (1988). *Power and criticism: Poststructural investigations in education*. New York: Teachers College Press.

Clark, D. L., & Astuto, T. A. (1994). Redirecting reform: Challenges to popular assumptions about teachers and students. *Phi Delta Kappan, 75*, 513–520.

Cochran-Smith, M., & Lytle, S. L. (1993). *Inside/outside: Teacher research and knowledge*. New York: Teachers College Press.

Collins, J. (2001). *Good to great*. New York: HarperCollins.

Cooperrider, D. L., & Whitney, D. L. (1999). *Appreciative inquiry: Collaborating for change*. San Francisco: Barrett-Koehler Communications.

Corcoran, T., Fuhrman, S. H., & Belcher, C. L. (2001). The district role in instructional improvement. *Phi Delta Kappan, 83*, 78–84.

Costa, A. L., & Garmston, R. J. (1994). *Cognitive coaching*. Norwood, MA: Christopher-Gordon Publishers.

Covey, S. (1989). *The seven habits of highly effective people: Restoring the character ethic*. New York: A Fireside Book.

Crisci, P., & Herpel, R. (1984). *Win/win: An anatomy of an alternative approach*. Kent, OH: Ohio Center for School Personnel Relations.

Cuban, L. (1992). What happens to reform that lasts? The case of the junior high school. *American Educational Research Journal, 32*, 227–251.

Danielson, C. (1996). *Enhancing professional practice: The framework for teaching*. Alexandria, VA: Association for Supervision and Curriculum Development.

Danielson, C., & McGreal, T. (2000). *Teacher evaluation to enhance professional practice*. Alexandria, VA: Association for Supervision and Curriculum Development.

Darling-Hammond, L. (1997). *The right to learn: A blueprint for creating schools that work*. San Francisco: Jossey-Bass.

Darling-Hammond, L., & McLaughlin, M. (1995). Policies that support professional development in an era of reform. *Phi Delta Kappan, 76*, 597–604.

Deal, T. E., & Peterson, K. D. (1999). *Shaping school culture: The heart of leadership.* San Francisco: Jossey-Bass.

DuFour, R., & Eaker, R. (1992). *Creating the new American school: A principal's guide to school improvement.* Bloomington, IN: National Educational Service.

Fayol, H. (1949). *General and industrial management.* London: Pitman.

Ferguson, M. (1980). *The Aquarian conspiracy: Personal and social transformation in the 1980s.* Los Angeles: J. P. Tarcher.

Follett, M. P. (1918). *The new state.* New York: Longmanns, Green and Company.

Follett, M. P. (1924). *Creative experience.* London, New York, Toronto: Longmanns, Green and Company.

Follett, M. P., Metcalf, H. C., & Urwick, L. F. (Eds.). (1941). *Dynamic administration: The collected papers of Mary Parker Follett.* New York: Harper.

Freeman, D. (1998). *Doing teacher research: From inquiry to understanding.* Pacific Grove, CA: Heinle & Heinle.

Fromm, E. (1947). *Man for himself.* New York: Fawcett.

Fujioka, K. (1998, September). The talking stick: An American Indian Tradition in the ESL classroom. *The Internet TESL Journal, IV*(9). Retrieved May 28, 2004, from http://iteslj.org/Techniques/Fujioka-TalkingStick.html

Fullan, M. (1993). *Change forces: Probing the depths of educational reform.* New York: Falmer.

Fullan, M. (1994). Teacher leadership: A failure to conceptualize. In D. R. Walling (Ed.), *Teachers as leaders: Perspectives on the professional development of teachers* (pp. 241–254). Bloomington, IN: Phi Delta Kappa Educational Foundation.

Fullan, M., & Hargreaves, A. (1996). *What's worth fighting for in your school?* New York: Teachers College Press.

Gardner, W. (1983). *A nation at risk.* Washington, DC: U.S. Government Printing Office.

Giancola, J. M. (1988). *A study of the implementation of program budgeting, cost accounting, and reporting in Ohio school districts.* Unpublished doctoral dissertation, Kent State University, Kent, Ohio.

Glasser, W. (1990). *The quality school.* New York: Harper & Row.

Glickman, C. D. (1995). *Action research: Inquiry, reflection, and decision-making* (video). Alexandria, VA: Association for Supervision and Curriculum Development.

Greene, M. (1991). Teaching: The question of personal reality. In A. Lieberman & L. Miller (Eds.), *Staff development for education in the '90s* (2nd ed.). New York: Teachers College Press.

Greenleaf, R. K. (1977). *Servant leadership.* New York/Mahwah, NJ: Paulist Press.

Greenleaf, R. K. (1998). *The power of servant-leadership.* San Francisco: Berrett-Koehler Publishers.

Hackney, C. E., Reading, D., & Runnestrand, D. (2000). *Struggling for authentic human synergy and a robust democratic culture: The wellspring community for women in education leadership.* Final report of a project funded by the Ontario Ministry of Education Transfer Grant. Toronto: Department of Educational Administration, Ontario Institute for Studies in Education.

Hall, G. (1995). The local educational change process and policy implementation. In D. Carter & M. O'Neill (Eds.), *International perspectives on educational reform and policy implementation* (pp. 101–121). London: Falmer Press.

Halliman, M. (Ed.). (1995). *Restructuring schools: Promising practices.* New York: Plenum Press.

Herman, J., & Herman, J. (1993). *School based management: Current thinking and practice.* Springfield, IL: Charles C Thomas.

Hersey, P., Blanchard, K., & Johnson, D. (1996). *Management of organizational behavior* (7th ed.). Englewood Cliffs, NJ: Prentice-Hall.

Hesse, H. (1956). *Journey to the east.* New York: Noonday Press.

Hord, S. M. (1995). The local educational change process and policy implementation. In D. Carter & M. O'Neill (Eds.), *International perspectives on educational reform and policy implementation* (pp. 86–100). London: Falmer Press.

Hord, S. M., Rutherford, W. L., Huling-Austin, L., & Hall, G. E. (1987). *Taking charge of change.* Alexandria, VA: Association for Supervision and Curriculum Development.

Hutchison, J. K. (1997). *A study of teacher reformers' perceptions of power relations.* Unpublished doctoral dissertation, Kent State University, Kent, Ohio.

Jourard, S. M. (1971). *The transparent self.* New York: D. Van Nostrand Company.

Jourard, S. M., & Lasakow, P. (1958). A research approach to self-disclosure. *Journal of Abnormal Psychology, 56*(1), 91–98.

Kegan, R. (1994). *In over our heads.* Cambridge, MA: Harvard University Press.

Kegan, R. (2000). What "form" transforms? A constructive-developmental approach to transformative learning. In J. Mezirow (Ed.), *Learning as transformation: Critical perspectives on a theory in progress* (pp. 35–69). San Francisco: Jossey-Bass.

King, R. A., Swanson, A. D., & Sweetland, S. R. (2003). *School finance: Achieving high standards with equity and efficiency* (3rd ed.). New York: Allyn & Bacon.

Knowles, M. S. (1980). *The modern practice of adult education: From pedagogy to andragogy* (2nd ed.). New York: Cambridge Books.

Kotter, J. (1996). *Leading change.* Boston: Harvard Business School Press.

Kreisberg, S. (1992). *Transforming power: Domination, empowerment, education.* Albany, NY: SUNY Press.

Lambert, L., Collay, M., Dietz, M. E., Kent, K., & Richert, A. E. (1996). *Who will save our schools? Teachers as constructivist leaders.* Thousand Oaks, CA: Corwin.

Lieberman, A. (1995). Practices that support professional development. *Phi Delta Kappan, 76,* 591–596.

Lipsitz, J. (1995). Prologue: Why should we care about caring. *Phi Delta Kappan, 76,* 665–666.

Lord, B. (1994). Teachers' professional development: Critical colleagueship and the role of professional communities. In N. Cobb (Ed.), *The future of education: Perspectives on national standards in America.* New York: College Entrance Examination Board.

MacGregor, D. (1960). *The human side of enterprise.* New York: McGraw-Hill.

Manitonquat (no first name). (2003, Winter). The talking circle. *What would democracy look like, Winter 2003.* Retrieved May 28, 2004, from http://www.futurenet.org/24democracy/manitonquat.htm

Maxcy, S. J. (1991). *Educational leadership: A critical pragmatic perspective.* New York: Bergin & Garvey.

May, R. (1972). *Power and innocence.* New York: Norton.

McCutcheon, G. (1995). *Developing the curriculum: Solo and group deliberation.* White Plains, NY: Longman.

Merriam, S. B., & Caffarella, R. S. (1991). *Learning in adulthood: A comprehensive Guide*. San Francisco: Jossey-Bass.

Merriam-Webster's Collegiate Dictionary (11th ed.). (2004). Springfield, MA: Merriam-Webster.

Mezirow, J. (1990). *Fostering critical reflection in adulthood: A guide to transformative and emancipatory education*. San Francisco: Jossey-Bass.

Mezirow, J. (2000). Learning to think like an adult: Core concepts of transformation theory. In J. Mezirow (Ed.), *Learning as transformation* (pp. 3–33). San Francisco: Jossey-Bass.

Miller, J. B. (1976). *Toward a new psychology of women*. Boston: Beacon Press.

Mills, G. E. (2003). *Action research: A guide for the teacher researcher* (2nd ed.). Upper Saddle River, NJ: Merrill Prentice Hall.

Minstrell, J. (1999). Expertise in teaching. In R. J. Sternberg & J. A. Horvath (Eds.), *Tacit knowing in professional practice: Researcher and practitioner perspectives* (pp. 215–230). Mahwah, NJ: Erlbaum.

Moore, G. K. (1993). *The adventure education center instructor's manual*. Columbus, OH: Direct Instructional Support Systems.

Motley, V. (2004). *A contextual analysis of team leader trust in Ohio middle schools and its relationship to student achievement*. Unpublished doctoral dissertation, University of Akron, Ohio.

Murphy, J. (1995). Restructuring schools in Kentucky. In K. Leithwood (Ed.), *Transforming politics into education*. Albany, NY: SUNY Press.

Murphy, J., & Beck, L. (1995). *School based management as school reform: Taking stock*. Thousand Oaks, CA: Corwin.

National Center for Education Statistics. (1997). *Third international mathematics and science study (TIMSS)*. Washington, DC: National Center for Education Statistics.

National Commission on Teaching and America's Future. (1996). *What matters most: Teaching for America's future*. Washington, DC: National Commission on Teaching and America's Future. Retrieved February 25, 2005, from http://www.nctaf.org/article/index

The New Lexicon Webster's Encyclopedic Dictionary (Deluxe Edition). (1990). New York: Lexicon Publications.

Noddings, N. (1992). *The challenge to care in schools*. New York: Teachers College Press.

Oden, H. W. (1999). Transforming the organization: A social-technical approach. Westport, CT: Quorum Books.

Ohio Department of Education. (2003). *What is standards-based education?* Retrieved July 29, 2003, from http://ims.ode.state.oh.us

Palmer, P. J. (1998). *The courage to teach: Exploring the inner landscape of a teacher's life*. San Francisco: Jossey-Bass.

Piaget, J. (1972). Intellectual evolution from adolescent to adulthood. *Human Development, 16,* 346–370.

Pinnell, G. S., & Wayson, W. W. (in draft form). *Helping children learn in failure-oriented systems*. Ohio State University.

Pogrow, S. (1996). Reforming the wanna be reformers: Why education reforms almost always end up making things worse. *Phi Delta Kappan, 77,* 656–663.

Popkewitz, T. S. (1991). *A political sociology of educational reform*. New York: Teachers College Press.

Putnam, R. D. (2000). Bowling alone: America's declining social capital. *Journal of Democracy, 6*(1), 65–78.

Raywid, M. A. (1993). Finding time for collaboration: *Educational Leadership, 51,* 30–34.

Rearick, M., & Feldman, A. (1999). Orientations, product, reflections: A framework for understanding action research. *Teaching and Teacher Education, 15*(4), 333–350.

Rich, A. (1976). *Of woman born.* New York: Norton.

Sagor, R. (1997). Collaborative action research for educational change. In A. Hargreaves (Ed.), *Rethinking educational change with heart and mind.* Alexandria, VA: Association for Supervision and Curriculum Development.

Sarason, S. B. (1990). *The predictable failure of educational reform.* San Francisco: Jossey-Bass.

Schaef, A. W., & Fassel, D. (1988). *The addictive organization.* San Francisco: Harper.

Schlechty, P. C. (1997). *Inventing better schools.* San Francisco: Jossey-Bass.

Schlechty, P. C. (2001). *Shaking up the school house: How to support and sustain educational innovation.* San Francisco: Jossey-Bass.

Sears, J. B. (1950). *The nature of the administrative process.* New York: McGraw-Hill.

Senge, P. (1990). *The fifth discipline: The art and practice of the learning organization.* New York: Doubleday Currency.

Sergiovanni, T. J. (1992). *Moral leadership: Getting to the heart of school improvement.* San Francisco: Jossey-Bass.

Sergiovanni, T. J. (1994). *Building community in schools.* San Francisco: Jossey-Bass.

Sizer, T. (1992). *Horace's compromise: The dilemma of the American school system.* Boston: Houghton Mifflin.

Sparks, D., & Hirsh, S. (1997). *A new vision of staff development.* Alexandria, VA: Association for Supervision and Curriculum Development.

Stacey, R. D. (2001). *Complex responsive processes in organizations: Learning and knowledge creation.* New York: Routledge.

Stogdill, R. M., & Coons, A. E. (1957). *Leader behavior: Its description and measurement* (Research Monograph No. 88). Columbus, OH: Ohio State University.

Struthers, R. (2002). *The experience of providing education on Type 2 diabetes in American Indian communities: Emotions and feelings.* Paper presented at the 2002 National Rural Women's Health Conference. Abstract retrieved June 25, 2005, from http://ruralwomenshealth.psu.edu/s07_rstruthers.html

Surrey, J. L. (1987). *Relationship and power.* Wellesley, MA: Stone Center Working Paper Series.

U.S. Census Bureau. (2002). *Number, timing, and duration of marriages and divorces: Fall 1996.* Washington, DC: U.S. Department of Commerce.

Vygotsky, L. (1962). *Thought and language.* Cambridge, MA: MIT Press.

Wangerin, W. (1984). *Ragman and other stories of faith.* New York: HarperCollins.

Watts, G. D., & Castle, S. (1993). The time dilemma in school restructuring. *Phi Delta Kappan, 75,* 306–310.

Weick, K. E. (1995). *Sensemaking in organizations.* Thousand Oaks, CA: Sage.

Wegenke, G. (1994). Reflections on systemic change in the Des Moines Public Schools. *Studies in Educational Evaluation, 20,* 69–86.

Wheatley, M. J. (1992). *Leadership and the new science: Learning about organization from an orderly universe.* San Francisco: Berrett-Koehler.

Whitehead, A. N. (1926). *Religion in the making.* New York: Fordham University Press.

Wiggins, G., & McTighe, J. (1998). *Understanding by design.* Alexandria, VA: Association for Supervision and Curriculum Development.

Wood, G. H. (1992). *Schools that work.* New York: Penguin Group.

Index